THE GERMAN PENETRATION OF SOE

Jean Overton Fuller

THE GERMAN
PENETRATION
OF SOE

Published by Sapere Books.

24 Trafalgar Road, Ilkley, LS29 8HH

United Kingdom

saperebooks.com

ISBN: 978-1-80055-759-8.

TABLE OF CONTENTS

FOREWORD

I have never been an agent, of SOE or of any other organisation. I spent the war entirely in London, for most of the time as an Examiner in the Postal Censorship. It was solely in order to trace the fate of one person that I started my researches into SOE. I knew the Inayat Khan family, and Noor Inayat Khan had served in SOE under the code-name of 'Madeleine'. Her unaccountable disappearance had caused her family unending concern. Enquiry into the fate of this one girl, whom I had known, brought me to the discovery of dark mysteries, nothing of which appeared in the glossy success stories published. It was these mysteries, which as they disclosed themselves to me layer after layer, gave me the material for my successive books. I came to know agents on both sides of the fence. There was a time when half my acquaintance seemed to be from this shadow world.

I had not meant to write more about SOE, but circumstances have conspired to bring me back to it. I wrote a letter to *The Times*, and out of the blue William Kimber wrote to me, asking if I would write a book for his firm on the subject of my researches.

In other books, I have drawn portraits in depth of individual agents, studied more psychologically. What Mr Kimber wanted of me, and I have endeavoured to present, is a drawing together of the many threads, showing the overall pattern, and I have given particular attention to the chain-formation lying behind the spread of arrests from one area to another.

INTRODUCTION

SOE (Special Operations Executive) was not under the direction of the Foreign Office or the War Office and was probably regarded uneasily by each. It was Churchill's baby, and responsible to the Cabinet through the Ministry of Economic Warfare. Why anything so adventurous should have been placed under the wing of this obscure Ministry is a question I have never seen asked, but Colonel Frank Spooner, head of the Security Training School, at Beaulieu, told me that in the beginning it undertook simply *coup de main* raids on particular factories and works in the countries occupied by the Germans, and so perhaps its sphere was then thought to be mainly economic. These were of a commando type; the men infiltrated had just to blow up something and come back.

Before long, however, agents were in some places being sent in to stay. Their tasks were twofold. On the one hand, they were to undertake pieces of particular sabotage; on the other, they were to receive and stockpile arms, munitions and equipment parachuted monthly, when the moon was large, so that they should be available to secret partisans of the Allies, who could, on D Day, rise and harry the Germans in the rear. To some extent, the immediate and long-term tasks were incompatible, for the sporadic acts of sabotage drew the attention of the Germans to the groups that organised them, whereas for the building up of the secret army anything that advertised the activity of its organisers risked its security. For the long-term objective what was needed, really, was secrecy until D Day; but in 1941, when the first agents were parachuted, D Day seemed remote as the moon.

The first Minister of Economic Warfare, to whom Churchill issued the historic injunction to 'set Europe ablaze' was Hugh Dalton. He was succeeded by Lord Selborne. Business, the city and money were, as Spooner pointed out to me, much to the fore in the higher echelons: Robin Brook (later Governor of the Bank of England). Sir Charles Hambro of Hambros Bank, David Keswick of Jardine Matheson, James Hutchison of the shipping line, Nathan Sporborg of Slaughter and May were names I took down from his dictation — and above all Courtaulds Ltd., from whom, he told me, SOE received very considerable financial donations. These names I have since seen[1] in the official history by Professor M.R.D. Foot[2] and I shall not attempt to sort out their exact involvement.

The military head of SOE was Brigadier, later Major-General, Sir Colin Gubbins, and beneath him it was divided out into different country sections. With regard to France, there were two sections concerned. One, RF (*République Française*) was, through its head, Hutchison, liaised with General de Gaulle's Free French Forces and directed by General Dewavrin, whose code-name was 'Passy'. Its agents were mostly French, though one of the most distinguished Englishmen, Wing-Commander F.F.E. Yeo-Thomas ('Shelley', 'White Rabbit') served in it. The other, which remained wholly under British control, was the French Section (F). The first

---

[1] It was after the publication of my second book on SOE, *The Starr Affair*, that, in August 1954, Colonel Spooner invited me to come and spend a few days with him and his wife at their home in the Channel Islands Bearing in mind his former function and the controversial nature of my book, I half wondered if the purpose for which I was being summoned was to be 'hauled over the coals' for having made public what had come to my knowledge. It was not that He was interested by my disclosures and proved a good friend to me.

[2] *SOE in France*, HM Stationery Office, 1966 Second edition with amendments 1968

head Brigadier Leslie Humphreys, who when he moved to the Escapes Section handed over to H.R. Marriott, former Courtaulds' representative in Paris; Marriott resigned, following a disagreement and was briefly succeeded by Thomas Cadett, of the BBC; he also resigned following a disagreement and was in September 1941 succeeded by Captain Maurice Buckmaster, later Lieut-Colonel, a temporary officer, formerly Ford's manager in Paris. Second in command to him was Major Nicholas Bodington, former Reuters Correspondent in Paris.

At any rate in the French Section and RF Section, all the men and women parachuted had officers' ranks, in the Army or Air Force. There were no 'other ranks' in these sections. They worked usually in teams of three, organiser, wireless operator and courier. The organiser was chief of the other two. The place of 'other ranks' was, in a sense, composed by the recruits they made in France, who were in their ensemble referred to as their network. These would be the people who helped tow and stow away parachute cargoes, allowed their homes to be used for wireless transmission or as letterboxes at which agents could leave and collect messages.

A Maquis was something different. Maquisards were men who had burned their bridges behind them and lived camped out in wild and mountainous districts. Their existence was hardly secret; they were simply too awkward to be worth the Germans' trouble to attempt to dislodge. But of course, there was a problem of conveying food as well as arms to them, and certain of those SOE Organisers who were operative in areas where there was a Maquis became chiefs of Maquis, commanders of veritable armies. A network in the ordinary sense, however, was composed of ordinary people, leading their otherwise ordinary lives in their own homes in the towns. Some networks were liaised with Maquis. Borderlines blurred.

There was also the Escapes Section, which crossed country boundaries, occupying itself with, for instance, escapes of shot down airmen or political persons from, say, Holland, via Belgium and France to Spain or Switzerland. This was direction by Colonel Leslie Humphreys, and was distinct from continental escape lines which worked to MI9.

All these organisations were supposed to be separate; yet one finds points in the story at which they impinge one on another.

All worked in plain clothes. All received only the ordinary pay of their rank.

Agents could be parachuted 'blind' (with no one to meet them) or to 'reception committee' (two or three people to meet them).

The German services the agents came up against were the Abwehr (Military Counter-Espionage), which was relatively more powerful at the beginning, and the SS service which later came to take over power increasingly from it. Initially lodged in the abandoned office of the Sûreté in the rue de Saussaies, this moved early in 1942 to the broad Avenue Foch, where it installed itself in Nos. 82 and 84; Sturmbannführer Boemelburg's department was in 82 and Sturmbannführer Kieffer's in 84. Most of what the public, and indeed the Resistance, called Gestapo was in fact Sicherheitsdienst, the abbreviation of which is SD, its HQ was Kieffer's department at 84 Avenue Foch, which received data sent up to it by subordinate SD HQs all over France, and took over from them the interrogation of major agents only. The lesser prisoners were still taken to the rue des Saussaies. Nevertheless, Ernst Vogt, Kieffer's interpreter, whom I came to know very well, wrote to me in his slightly broken English:[3]

What concerns the popular error about the Gestapo in France, it is really very difficult to explain. You cannot say that there was no Gestapo in France. There was a political section of the Sicherheitspolizei which was called 'Gestapo', the chief of it was the SS Sturmbannführer Boemelburg.... Our service had nothing to do with this section, but was nevertheless under its direction as Boemelburg was also the chief of Kieffer. The SD was a special section of the Sicherheitspolizei, it was the intelligence service. Sicherheitspolizei (Gestapo) and SD were all together under the same direction of the RHSA (Reichssicherheitshauptamt) Berlin.

---

[3] Vogt, letter to author, September 28, 1950.

I: EARLY NETWORKS PARIS AND MARSEILLES

The first agent parachuted by the French section was Georges Bégué, alias 'Georges Noble', dropped blind near Châteauroux on the night of March 5/6,[4] 1941. This pioneer was his own radio operator. Sent by Thomas Cadett, then second in command to Marriott, he presented himself to a friend of Cadett's, Max Hymans, who agreed to help him; he introduced him to people, including one Fleuret, a garage-keeper, who agreed to become the first letterbox. Bégué was able to pave the way for the next three agents, who were dropped on May 10/11, Pierre de Vomécourt ('Lucas'), Roger Cottin ('Albert') and one 'Bernard', who was denounced to Vichy police by French peasants who had seen him land and defected to the service of Vichy.[5] Pierre de Vomécourt enlisted his brother Philippe ('Gauthier').

In July, RF infiltrated its first agents into Normandy and Brittany. Jean Moulin, destined to be its towering figure, arrived in London, from France, in October.[6]

De Guelis of the French Section and Gilbert Turck ('Christophe') were parachuted by the August moon.[7] De

---

[4] A night begins on the evening of one day and ends during the early morning of the next Dates of night operations are given here as normally by SOE agents with both their starting and finishing day-dates

[5] *SOE in France*, M.R.D. Foot (HM Stationery Office 1966), hereinafter referred to as the Official History, pp 162-63

[6] Official History, p 166.

[7] August 6 according to the Official History, p. 169; August 8 according to Turck's statement to me

Guelis made important recruits in France, Dr Levy of Antibes, Philippe Liewer, Francis Garel, Robert Lyon and an American lady, Virginia Hall. A Lysander aircraft deposited Gerard ('Jerry') Morel on the evening of September 4.[8] On September 6/7 were parachuted Benjamin Cowburn, Michael Trotobas, Victor Gerson (destined to become the chief figure of Escapes Section), George Langelaan, the Comte du Puy and Georges Bloch. On September 19 Francis Basin ('Olive'), Leroy, Roche and Dubourdin were landed from HMS *Fidelity*,[9] and on the night of October 10/11 were parachuted J. B. Hayes, Jumeau, Le Harivel and Turberville.

This completes the cast at the moment when the first major blow fell.

The blow engendered 'the affair of the Villa des Bois'. I came on it, as I came on all SOE mysteries, by chance. That is to say, when I was between my second and third books, Yeo-Thomas said to me that as I was dealing with 'peculiar mysteries' perhaps I would like another. He had just received a letter from a friend of his, Gilbert Turck, asking if he could not hasten the issue of his case, which was so complicated it would be better Turck told me about it himself. Yeo-Thomas was sure Turck's unforgiven offence was after the war to have refused to divide with Pierre de Vomécourt a large packet of banknotes which had been parachuted out during the war, and

---

[8] Official History, p 171

[9] Professor Foot includes R B Roche amongst those landed from *Fidelity* (Official History, p 173), but Henri Noguères refers to a document on the files of the *Comite d'Histoire de la Deuxième Guerre Mondiale* showing that Raymond Roche was landed on the beach at Cannet on August 25/26 and made contact with Bégué at Chateauroux forty-eight hours afterwards; *Histoire de la Resistance en France, 1940-1945*, Henri Noguères in collaboration with M Degliame-Fouche and J.L Vigier (Laffont, Paris, 1969), Vol I, p 119n.

to have handed the packet in at the British Embassy. Barbara Yeo-Thomas, listening, commented, 'The British Embassy must have fainted!', and Yeo-Thomas added that such private division of unused funds was so frequent one could almost say it was habitual. What was unusual was the malevolence with which Turck had been persecuted by de Vomécourt. He telephoned Turck and asked him to receive me.

I called on Turck and his wife on January 24, 1955. Turck made a good impression on me, slight of build but with eagle-clear eyes. Only, from the eagerness with which he received me, I felt he assumed because I had come from Yeo-Thomas that I was someone who, if satisfied, could do something towards obtaining his *blanc-seing*. I had to disabuse him, but he told me his story all the same, and I recapitulate it from the pencilled notes I made while he was talking.

In March 1940 Turck came to know Colonel Humphreys at the Cinquième Bureau (counter-espionage department), of the Ecole Militaire, where he was taught about explosives and sabotage. When France fell, in June of that year, Humphreys asked him to go with him to England. He would have left with Humphreys, but that he was wounded and had to remain for a while in the Val de Grace Hospital; he followed Humphreys after a short delay, leaving from Bordeaux St. Jean de Luz with a party of Poles on June 25, 1940. On his arrival in England, he enlisted on July 1 in the Free French Forces. Later, Humphreys proposed to him that he should return to France as his own representative, and on August 8 he was parachuted near Montluçon, with the code-name 'Christophe' and instructions to contact a Commandant Brecheu and others, and to organise arms-dumps.

He took a villa in Marseilles, called the Villa des Bois, and began organising arms-dumps. Some he organised in the area of Châteauroux, in conjunction with Georges Bégué. On October 2 he met in Marseilles Pierre de Vomécourt, and shortly afterwards he met at the Café Colisée in Paris Philippe de Vomécourt. He moved backwards and forwards across the demarcation line between the Unoccupied and Occupied Zones. On October 3 he left Marseilles for Paris by a train carrying soldiers repatriated from Syria. He travelled almost officially. In Paris he met Pierre de Vomécourt at the Café Colisée.

On behalf of Humphreys Turck now organised an escape-line from the German Occupied to the Unoccupied Zone of France, from Paris to Marseilles. About October 17 he chanced to meet a certain Méglé, who put him in touch with Roland Leguy, who promised him a German safe conduct for 5,000 francs. Philippe de Vomécourt had a German identity card; a safe conduct would obviously be useful. The one which Méglé produced was, however, so poorly faked that Turck refused to buy it. Méglé appeared as much angered by the inept work as himself, perhaps because he had hoped for a percentage. But in fact Méglé turned out later to have been a German agent.

About October 20, Turck intended returning to Marseilles. However, he broke his journey at Lyons, where he contacted a Commandant Zundel. Zundel told him the Villa des Bois had been occupied by the Vichy police and that some people had been arrested, and said, 'Be careful. Your description has been circulated throughout the area, and police are at the Villa des Bois.'

Turck returned to Paris and told Pierre de Vomécourt, who said they must inform England.

What had happened was that the Villa des Bois, having been detected as a Resistance safe-house, had been used as a mousetrap. Quite how it had been detected has in itself been debated. Apparently, though this he knew only after the war, one of the four agents parachuted on October 10/11, Tuberville, had been dropped wide of the others and arrested the following morning, and it was at first thought the address of the Villa des Bois must have been found on him. According, however, to the official report, made in 1946 by Wybot (Roger de Warin) in his function as director of the DST (*Département de la Surveillance du Territoire*, the department which after the war examined cases of suspected treason, before referring them, if it found cause, to the civilian or military justice), Turberville did not come into it and the affair had a different origin. It was 'Bouguennec' (Garel), who, having been arrested on October 9 at the Fleuret garage, gave his interrogators the address of Christophe, Villa des Bois, which led to the arrest of Jumeau on October 17 and Bloch on October 20, when they called there, and of the tenant of the nearby Villa Bernadette when he called there; this person, says Wybot's statement, was released but watched, and it was at the Villa Bernadette that Lyon called, looking vainly for Turck, and was given the rendezvous at the restaurant where he was arrested, as was Hayes, who went to it with him. De Harivel, likewise, went to the Villa Bernadette and was given the café rendezvous at which he was arrested on October 24; Turck had left for the Occupied Zone on October 3 in a convoy of repatriated soldiers.

Wybot's statement does not mention the most important of the agents arrested, Bégué, on October 24.

All of the agents arrested in this affair later escaped, Turberville from a train and the rest on July 16, 1942, from the prison at Mausac.

There was a period during which Turck did not see Pierre de Vomécourt, and for a reason of which he could not have dreamed. On December 28, 1941, de Vomécourt was introduced by a Maître Brault, to an attractive, intelligent woman Mathilde-Lily Carré, whose code-name was '*La Chatte*', 'the Cat'. What he did not know was that when he met her she was a prisoner.

Together with a Pole, Roman Czerniawski, she had been chief of an independent organisation, the Interallié, which sent intelligence to London. The network had been penetrated when a man employed in the harbour at Cherbourg reported to the Abwehr that a strange woman had been asking him questions about ship movements. This was not the Cat, but one of the local sub-agents. Captain Borchers of the Abwehr set out from Paris at once, and at Cherbourg took on a local Abwehr NCO, Sergeant Hugo Bleicher, to assist him. They arrested the woman.

Bleicher's methods from now on are significant to study. Guessing that the contact to whom she gave her information was her lover, he told her that this man, who set her to a task which imperilled her life, was deceiving her with women in Caen and in Paris; she was so overcome that she told them where she was next to meet the man, which enabled them to arrest him. Bleicher then told the man, who proved to be Raoul Kiffer, known as Kiki, that it was the woman he loved, oy whom he had been betrayed; and Kiki in his turn was so overcome that he gave away his own contact in Paris. In this way, playing one off against another, Bleicher penetrated higher into the organisation and in the small hours of November 18, 1941, they were able to arrest Czerniawski, together with the latter's mistress, Renée Borni. During the daylight hours of the same morning the Cat was apprehended in the street nearby, identified by a nod from Renée Borni.

To the best of my knowledge, I am the only private person to have seen an unpublished typescript by the Cat herself, *Mémoires d'une Chatte*, containing a good deal of material deleted from her later published memoirs, *I was the Cat* (Souvenir Press, 1959) and not made available to Gordon Young, author of *Cat with Two Faces* (Putnam, 1957). She is always frank about being a woman who has slept with a number of men, but there is in the typescript a detail which has, unaccountably, disappeared from the published version, namely that she did not sleep with Czerniawski, who was 'a friend, not a lover'; she uses the word *ami* in a rather un-French sense to make the distinction. I incline to accept this; nevertheless, I do not doubt that Bleicher exploited to the full the slight dislike existing between the colleague and the mistress, setting one against the other, and that to the Cat, in particular, he made the most of the fact that she was the victim at the end of a long line of betrayals. At any rate, her morale was completely sapped, and she was obliged to keep her appointments with other agents so that they could be arrested.

One of these was a young man, just eighteen, Claude Jouffret, who had been her lover, and whom, at the Café Louis XIV on December 5, she identified to Bleicher by greeting him with a kiss. It was this kiss of Judas, he was later to tell a court, which overthrew him. Moreover, I have indirect but very powerful testimony, from Henri Déricourt (see later chapters), who after the war shared his home with Jouffret and was the recipient of confidences, concerning the nature of the sexual intimacies alleged to have taken place between the Cat and Bleicher on the morning following her arrest; and I have no doubt that Bleicher did tell these things to Jouffret, the more thoroughly to complete his demoralisation. For Jouffret, too, now became helpless clay in Bleicher's hands.

When de Vomécourt first met the Cat, Bleicher was at the next table. But de Vomécourt, thinking a café not a good place to talk, suggested she come to his office. Bleicher had no choice but to let her go; so she saw de Vomécourt alone; and came clean.

De Vomécourt and Cowburn had been looking for a new radio operator. In fact, the Cat's radio was now being worked to London by the Germans, and it was the misleading intelligence sent over it, by a captured radio operator, to the effect that the three German ships, *Gneisenau, Scharnhorst* and *Prinz Eugen*, in Brest harbour for repairs, would not for long be able to put to sea, which in London overrode the correct intelligence sent by Colonel 'Rémy' of RF, and also by the Alliance organisation, that the repairs were completed and departure from port imminent, and so was responsible for the ships' being able to escape, unopposed.

But now a plan was evolved according to which the Germans were to connive at the escape of the Cat and de Vomécourt to London, in the belief she would spy for them. At the first attempt to fetch them by MTB the dinghy overturned, and two SOE agents, Redding and Abbot, stranded, were taken prisoner. But on the night of February 26/27, they were successfully collected. Bodington was on the MTB and they spent the first night in his flat — while a flat in Porchester Gate was fitted with concealed microphones. I have been unofficially informed that practically the only thing of interest the listeners-in heard was some adverse comments upon their own efficiency.

De Vomécourt was parachuted back on April 1, and gave Turck money from London for the escape route, and presented to him one Léon Wolters, a Belgian. Meanwhile, Jouffret had been set to shadow Cottin, and reported to

Bleicher that Cottin had met someone looking like de Vomécourt. Wolters was arrested on April 24 and gave away his rendezvous with de Vomécourt on the following day, April 25, on which de Vomécourt was arrested and according to the sworn evidence of Hugo Bleicher, given in a German court of law after the war, betrayed eight of his comrades in return for a promise that both he and they should be kept in a military POW camp instead of a Concentration Camp, which promise was kept: see the issues of *Die Frankfurter Allgemeine Zeitung, Bild* and other German newspapers for April 21, 1959.

Turck knew nothing of the involvement of Wolters, but distrusted him. He affected a limp, but when Madame Turck saw him in the street he was not limping. Madame Turck received a letter from Wolters, dated May 1, offering his services at 6,000 francs a month. Turck so strongly suspected him of being a German agent that he not only did not pay him 6,000 a month, he made plans to kill him and drop him in the Seine in a sack. However, Wolters did not make contact with them again.

The letter from Wolters to Madame Turck, which he showed me, was a capital document in his file, because some persons had alleged he was in the employ of Wolters, and this paper made it plain it was otherwise.

Turck was arrested on July 7, 1942, badly beaten, and sent to Compiègne, then to Buchenwald, and from there to Dora, an Extermination Camp, which he was lucky to survive. On his return to Paris after the war he handed in at the British Embassy the packet of money he had received from de Vomécourt; he showed me the receipt, together with the clearance he had received in London, signed by N.C. Mott and dated March 27, 1947.

In his own country, Turck was nevertheless now finding himself assailed by a strange allegation, that he had been inside the Villa des Bois during the time it was being used as a mousetrap and said 'Come in' to the others through the entryphone, and that he had no genuine mission from the British, but conducted a non-existent 'network' in the pay of Wolters. He was invited to attend a kind of non-legal court or Jurie d'Honneur without officiality, which he found to be composed only of accusers, including Philippe de Vomécourt. This took place in the Caserne de la Pépinière on March 18, 1947. Turck presented what he thought should be sufficient proofs of his innocence (though as he had never been charged before the law it was not for him to prove his innocence), but on the application of de Vomécourt and others the Ministre des Anciens Combattants struck him off the register and deprived him of all his rights as an ancient combatant. That was on March 25, 1947. Turck had two months in which to accept or appeal against the Minister's decision. He appealed at once, but at the time of our meeting, eight years afterwards, in 1955, he was still waiting for a decision. That was why he had written to Yeo-Thomas asking if he could not hasten matters.

By an odd chance, just after my return to London after this meeting with Turck I met a Miss Dorothy Duncan, who as secretary to the Chairman of Shell had been on the fringes of SOE, and she told me that shortly after the ending of the war, in 1945, Colonel Humphreys telephoned her and invited her to dinner. With him he had Turck and Madame Turck. Introducing them, he told her he had had great difficulty in rescuing Turck from something that seemed very nasty, and but for the intervention of Sir Frank Soskice did not know how he would have been able. The dinner was apparently to celebrate Turck's deliverance — but this was before he went back to the trouble in France.

There was to be a sequel. On February 25, 1959, the Tribunal de l'Administration Française overthrew the decision of the Ministre des Anciens Combattants, and Turck was restored to his rights and titles.

Pushed by de Vomécourt and others, the Minister appealed against the quashing of his decision.

On January 23, 1963, the highest authority in the land, the Conseil d'Etat, sustained the judgement of the Tribunal de l'Administration Française, assuring the Minister that Turck was an authentic Resistant, with nothing to his dishonour; and on his sixty-first birthday, March 26, 1972, at his birthplace, Frestoy-Vaux, of which he was already Mayor, the Grand-Commander of the Legion d'Honneur, Marcel Dessault, created Turck Commander of the Legion of Honour. On February 8, 1975, I met Colonel Humphreys; he assured me Turck was 'brave, loyal and true'.

There is one treason which, though not within SOE, was to impinge upon it. In the summer of 1941 there appeared in the north of France an apparently attractive figure, tall, with red hair, Captain Paul Cole of the Royal Engineers; he was, he told people, a British Intelligence agent, formerly a Scotland Yard detective, who had remained behind after the evacuation of the BEF from Dunkirk in order to help British and Allied soldiers who found themselves stranded. Actually, his name was Harold Cole, he was a Sergeant, not a Captain, in the Royal Engineers, and his only connection with Scotland Yard was his record at it as a con man. Nevertheless, if the picture he presented of himself was brightened with false touches, there is no doubt that he did, in the beginning, genuinely help stranded soldiers and shot-down airmen to escape. He established himself at Lille, where he worked principally with a hairdresser, Madame Voglicimacci, and a couple called Duprez.

Soon he came to be in contact with Ian Garrow, founder of what later came to be known as the *Pat* escape line, based on Marseilles, working to MI9. 'Lieutenant Commander Pat O'Leary, RN' was the pseudonym of a Belgian army doctor, Albert Guérisse, generally known as 'Pat'. In November 1941, Pat realised that Cole, who had been drawing money from *Pat* in order, he said, to pay Duprez, was not paying Duprez, but on the contrary borrowing from him. Cole was tackled by Pat, Bruce Dowding and Mario Prassino. Pat, in front of Cole, said he thought they ought to kill him. Prassino, horrified, protested that death was too heavy a penalty for embezzlement. The point was, of course, that an untrustworthy man was dangerous, and if they were not to kill him it was difficult to know what else to do with him. Cole was locked into the bathroom while the question was further discussed, and escaped out of the bathroom window.

It was unfortunate that this occurred just before Cole was arrested by the Germans, on or before December 11, 1941. How he would have withstood interrogation had his relations with his colleagues been happy, we cannot know; but having been worse than cast out by Pat, there was no incentive for him to be steadfast. The people whom he gave away, however, were not those who had menaced him, relatively safe in the Vichy zone, but those in the German occupied zone who, because of the difficulty of contacts, did not know that he had been written off by Pat; these included the priest who made out false identity cards for escaping Allied soldiers and airmen.

Cole does seem to have had a revulsion from his treason, for after a few days he fled from the Germans to Susanne Warenghem, a young member of the organisation. Unaware he had betrayed everyone with whom he was in contact, she hid him, in the home of one of her aunts, and was later married to him by a priest.

Susanne Warenghem came to see me at my flat on March 5, 1959, and told me her entire story. This was before she met her eventual biographer, Gordon Young. From the details she gave me, nervous and troubled, the picture which emerged really was one of a natural crook; he even stole her aunt's silver, money and jewellery, and, when she told him she was about to bear his child, gave her a genuine plan of a German aerodrome to present to a 'Resistant' who was actually a German agent. This was revealed to her by a kindly Vichy police inspector who, by arresting them both, certainly saved her life; for had she presented that paper she would have found herself in German hands.

Cole remained in prison in Vichy hands until the eventual occupation of the Vichy zone by the Germans.

One of the major agents of RF Section, perhaps indeed Dewavrin's most important agent, was Colonel Renault, better known under his eventual code-name, 'Rémy'. By March 1941 he had established a network in Bordeaux and another in Brest. The ban on real espionage in the French Section plainly did not operate in RF, for Rémy's activity was mainly one of organising the collection of intelligence, particularly marine intelligence, concerning activities in these two important ports. Moreover he was in contact with L'Alliance, an independent French network that was occupied purely with the collection of intelligence and sent its information to a quarter in London that was not SOE. The creator of L'Alliance, Loustaunau-Lacau was arrested on July 18, 1941, and a woman, Marie-Madeleine Méric (later Fourcade), code-name 'Hedgehog', took over the command of it. Rémy learned only later that in Bordeaux on the same day and the days following there were arrests in Bordeaux, though not of agents in direct contact with him.

Rémy had, in particular, kept an interested watch upon the three German battleships, *Scharnhorst*, *Gneisenau* and *Prinz Eugen* ever since they were being brought into Brest harbour for repairs, noting the stages in the re-making seaworthy, and had sent radio-telegrammes to London on February 1 and again on February 7, 1942, warning that they were likely to put out from port at the coming new moon — L'Alliance also warned through its own channels that departure of the cruisers was imminent. But unfortunately London preferred the comforting assurance of their unseaworthiness by the Germans, sent over the Cat radio, and also through a Dutch double-agent working for Colonel Giskes and took no action; hence the escape of the ships, which so enraged the British public. (It would have been more enraged had it known correct intelligence had been sent.)

Rémy's network was, however, to hatch out its own evil demon. By October 1941 the liaison between two of Rémy's agents, 'Espadon' (Jean Fleuret) and 'Moineau', was being made by a new courier, a young man of about twenty, with black hair, good-looking in a weak way, Pierre Cartaud, code-name 'Capri'.[10] Really, he should never have been recruited at all, for his father Captain Georges Cartaud was a collaborator, serving with the Germans on the Russian front in the LVF (Legion of French Volunteers against the Bolsheviks). Espadon, however, vouched for him; his views were not his father's, he was estranged from his father; Espadon had for

---

[10] There is a photograph of him in Rémy's *Livre du Courage et de la Peur*, I studied this in the French edition but there is an English translation published under the title *Courage and Fear* (Barker, 1950)

years treated him as his own son, Marc, who was Pierre Cartaud's best friend. When Espadon obtained possession of a piece of a new synthetic metal which was being manufactured in great secrecy, he broke it in half: half for himself to take to Rémy and half for Cartaud, to take to Rémy, should anything happen to himself. Thus, Cartaud came to know an address of Rémy, if not before. Perhaps it should have been foreseen that a young boy, however much estranged from his father, might under stress revert to the paternal pattern.

When Dewavrin ordered Rémy to come back to London, in June 1941, Espadon, trusting, confided Cartaud to him and asked him to take him with him. But just then a new wave of arrests occurred, two of those arrested being Rémy's sisters, and it quickly became apparent the Germans knew everything about Rémy, his true identity, his Paris address and habitual points of call. Before he left for London, Rémy knew who was to blame.

Cartaud had been arrested on the demarcation line. At that moment, his father, returned from the Russian front, wearing his German decorations, was back in Bordeaux; and it has been suggested he intervened on behalf of his son. According to a sister of Cartaud, he four times attempted suicide in his cell before he 'went over'.[11] It has been pointed out that four times is a lot, and that Cartaud's stay in prison was short. Whatever the anguished struggles which may have taken place in Cartaud's mind during the hours of transition, when he went over it was with an appearance of apparent animosity against all the Resistants with whom he had worked and by whom he had been trusted. Rémy added up a total of exactly sixty members of his network arrested through his agency. These

---

[11] I cannot recall my source for this; it was from a French paper I read while in France.

included the wife of Espadon. Espadon escaped, though only for the moment; he had altered his timetable and so failed to fall into the trap; but when he was arrested afterwards, in his civil identity as Jean Fleuret, it was Cartaud who told the Germans it was Espadon whom they had caught.

Ernst Vogt, Kieffer's interpreter, told me that from the time Cartaud was attached to their department he was determined to be more German than the Germans. He wished to be called not Pierre but Peter, pronounced in the German way; and he asked for his service with the SD to be counted towards his German naturalisation after the war. He was trusted to the point of being allowed to take the train to Bordeaux and come back by himself. He devoted himself to the German service with a 'zeal', Vogt told me, that left even the Germans slightly mystified. 'A bit of a swine.'

His attentions were not destined to be limited to what had been Rémy's network. We shall encounter him again in connection with the French Section.

II: 1942 RIVIERA NETWORKS

Francis Basin — he was French but when we met assured me he had been baptised with the English form of his Christian name — code-name 'Olive', one of the agents landed in the south of France from HMS *Fidelity*, was arrested by the Vichy police as a suspect within twenty-fours hours of his arrival; however, they were really not anxious to assist the Germans and affected to believe his cover-story and let him go. This was not too happy a start, as where there has been an arrest, there is always the possibility of the once arrested person's being remembered and his activities noted. However, Basin now established a network on the Riviera coast; the code-name of the network was *Urchin*. Before long, he was in contact with 'Carte'.

Carte was the pseudonym of the painter, André Girard, who, living at Antibes, was a neighbour of Dr Levy, the recruit of de Guelis. Girard's contacts were, for an artist, surprising, being nearly all amongst officers of the armistice army. He was in touch with General de Lattre de Tassigny and Colonel Vautrin, as well as with Captains Maurice Chevance and Henri Frenay, sometimes cited as the two first officers to become secret Resistants, and, notably, with le Commandant Henri Frager, an Alsatian who had served in World War I and had been in the French army in Algeria before a British submarine returned him to his native land. He became Girard's second in command. Other contacts of Girard were Guillain de Benouville and the left wing-poet, Emmanuel d'Astier de la Vigerie, destined to found the Libération movement. On the whole, however, it must be said that Girard's contacts seem to have been with the officer caste. His dream was the creation within the armistice army, allowed to Pétain by Hitler, of an army secretly pro-Allied; his idea was that, benefiting already from an ordered organisation, such a secret army within the army would prove a much more effective instrument for use when the time came than the Resistance movements springing up from among other elements of the population which de Gaulle (in Britain) hoped to unite under the leadership of his appointed representative in France — this was eventually to be Jean Moulin.

Presumably because of Basin's reports, in mid-January 1942 Peter Churchill was landed, by submarine on a brief mission, the aim of which was simply to meet Girard, alias Carte, find what he was like and discuss what, in practical terms, he could do. For it became quickly obvious in London that if Girard could do all he claimed, then he was a very big man indeed; he was offering nothing less than an alternative way of working than through de Gaulle.

In March, in the streets of Cannes, Basin ran into the Baron de Malval, whom he had known at the French Embassy in London. De Malval placed at Basin's disposal, and at the disposal of the British Government, his rented Villa d'Isabelle, just outside Cannes, and this became the headquarters of *Urchin*, and the safehouse which agents arriving from London in the south of France made their first place of call.

In August, Nicholas Bodington came out from London to hold deepened discussions with Girard about the potentialities of his organisation and the help it would require from London; Bodington stayed with de Malval at the Villa Isabelle.

By this time the elements Girard (Carte) had gathered around him were all beginning to quarrel. The quarrels within *Carte* are of an inconceivable complexity, which would be depressing to follow in detail. Very broadly, what happened was what might be expected; the left split off from the right. This Girard, who claimed to be non-political, in vain tried to prevent, in the name of unity against the Germans. It must be said, however, that personal rivalries were in transparent evidence.

Not only did Girard's own people quarrel; Basin now found it virtually impossible to work in collaboration with Girard. Part of the difficulty was of a nature to be found repeating itself in SOE history. Basin was the man from London, the SOE organiser with a rank and an authority from London. Girard was the self-constituted chief on the spot; he had no formal authority to give orders to SOE agents, yet London was treating him as a big man, so that when Basin saw a chance to organise a piece of railway sabotage near Marseilles and Girard vetoed it, as likely to compromise security, Basin gave up the project, but with violent resentment. Only personality, he maintained, had underlain Girard's veto; the project had been put down because it had not come from Girard.

The Baron de Malval, when he talked to me about the great Girard/Basin quarrel, lamented. He stayed with Basin, naturally, as he had known him in England and was his recruit; yet he felt the Resistance had been weakened by this schism. It was not a formal schism; the two camps still maintained formal relations, but in a glacial spirit.

Bodington, nevertheless, was impressed by Carte and amongst the projects discussed was a broadcasting station to be started in London, of which Claude Dauphin, the French film actor, should be the head. Professor Foot has written in the Official History[12] (much of which Girard has strongly challenged in one of his letters to me) that Carte's existence 'exercised a dominating influence' over the French Section's

---

[12] pp 204-05

work in 1942, as it seemed that he could prepare an army 300,000 strong, but that he never got further with it than listing the adherents.

Probably the simple discovery of adherents did seem to Girard the most pressing task, but the danger of his organisation lay in his list-making. Moreover, this was no mere list of names; beneath each name was an ample documentation concerning the person. There was reason for this amplitude. A recruit's first account of himself, taken down in detail, could be used to check his subsequent utterances for any discrepancy such as would give away an *agent provocateur*'s cover-story. These files constituted a risk, should they fall into enemy hands; but those who expressed concern were assured they were all ciphered, that they were not kept in Girard's house but dispersed through the homes of other members of the network, and that each lot was kept in a case, electrically fitted so that if opened in an improper way the contents would burn.

In mid-August Basin was arrested, and this time it was a serious arrest.

A few days afterwards Peter Churchill parachuted back, on the night of August 27/28 near Montpellier, this time with the codename 'Raoul'. On the same night, near Valence, John Starr, codename 'Emile', parachuted, and later described his arrival to me.

He took the train to Cannes, where as he descended from the train he hid himself in a French family, so as not to be noticeable as a single passenger, until he had got out of the railway station. He had now to find the Villa Isabelle, on the Route de Fréjus, and took a velo-taxi, a bicycle pulling a basket-chair on wheels. Arriving, he mistook for the villa what was only the lodge, of which he had not been told. He asked the porter for the Baron de Malval and was told he was out.

'But I'm expected,' said Starr. 'Do you mind if I go in?'

He found the far grander building within the grounds, but there was obviously nobody at home. He sat down and waited for some hours. About midnight, a glowing cigarette came up the drive.

The smoker of the cigarette, as he took shape in the darkness, said in English, 'What the hell are you doing here?'

It was Peter Churchill. Then a second glowing cigarette appeared. The man holding it was Major Nicholas Bodington. They had both been down to Cannes railway station to meet him, but because of his managing to look like part of the French family, had missed him and spent hours wondering where he had got to.

They took him into the magnificent villa, where he was given a beautiful bedroom with private bath attached. As his lack of sunburn gave him away as not a resident of the coast, they suggested to him that he lie about in the grounds to brown, before being conducted to Carte. He was taken to be introduced to Carte at a rehearsal of *Poile de Garotte*. Girard (Carte) had chosen this rendezvous because his daughter, later to become better known under her professional name as a film actress, Daniele Delorme, was playing the leading role in it, which made it natural for him to be there and to be talking to all kinds of people.

It was Girard who had asked London to send him a food expert, who would concern himself with the feeding of the Maquis camped out in the mountains back from the coast. Starr had protested in London, when picked for this job, that he knew nothing about food; and he was embarrassed at having to try to bluff Girard, 'the big chief'. However, perhaps because Starr was in civilian life a poster artist, he got on perfectly all right with the serious artist, Girard.

Afterwards he was taken to Antibes, and given a room in one of the safe-houses there. That evening his hostess took him round to a sculptor next door, to listen to the BBC and announced to the listening circle, '*C'est un Anglais. Il vient d'arriver par parachute.*' The sculptor was a member of the network and gave lessons in the handling of explosives, but the others were probably just friends. As one of those present was deaf, the information was repeated. Although the villa was back from the road, Starr felt worried by this insecurity, because somebody could easily have crept up through the grounds. How did they know there was not somebody crouching outside the window?

Later, he went with some members of the network to retrieve a food parcel parachuted with him which he had had to abandon because it was too awkward to transport; they found the container, but when they opened it, it proved to be filled with tinned foods in English wrappers, and chocolate in English wrappers. To be caught with this would prove connection with England.

In September word got round that Basin was being transferred from the local prison to one at Lyons and plans were made to rescue him. Peter Churchill, with assistants, was to snatch him from his guards as he was taken through Cannes railway station. If he failed, then Girard's men were to snatch him and haul him off the train at some convenient point between Cannes and Lyons; organisation of this reserve plan was delegated by Girard to Frager, who did not, however, form one of the action party. In fact, neither team succeeded in its job. Basin was led across Cannes railway station in front of Peter Churchill and his little force without their making a move — either the force guarding Basin looked to them too strong or they were just too slow to realise the moment was now — and the Girard-Frager team on the train also attempted nothing. Who was most to blame for this fiasco, Peter Churchill, Girard or Frager has been long and bitterly debated; what seems plain is that they failed between them because none was resolute.

Isadore Newman ('Julian'), who had been Basin's radio operator, was now transmitting for Peter Churchill and Girard, but went on strike over the length of the messages Girard required him to transmit. He had security sense on his side, for length of message increased likelihood of pin-pointing by the enemy. Peter Churchill, however, sustained Girard, so Newman quarrelled with him too, and asked London to bring him home. Luckily for Peter Churchill, someone at this moment introduced to him Adolphe Rabinovitch, ('Arnaud') a French Section wireless operator who had been dropped into the Grenoble area but who had not been able to find the people for whom he was supposed to work. Churchill obtained permission from London to keep him in Newman's place. Rabinovitch, a Russian-Egyptian Jew, tough and rough, was devoted to work, possessed of a shrewd good sense, and courageous; one of the best individuals SOE put into the field.

Peter Churchill next began to quarrel with Girard, while his relations with de Malval, in whose house he was living also deteriorated.

The October felucca brought John Goldsmith ('Valentin'), Sidney Jones ('Felix') and Chalmers Wright of the Political Warfare Department. They were received on the beach by Frager and André Marsac ('End'). It is good to be able to say that Goldsmith found Girard 'a man of immense charm'.[13]

---

[13] *Accidental Agent*, John Goldsmith (Leo Cooper, 1971), p 44 Unlike so many SOE memoirs, this book smacks of modesty, charm and good humour, perhaps these were the qualities which enabled him to

The November felucca, by which John Starr went home, in company with Claude Dauphin, brought seven passengers, one of whom was John's elder brother, George Starr, destined to become one of the few SOE organisers to achieve the objective of bringing his Maquis into action to greet D Day. It was a strange moment for the brothers, neither of whom had known the other was in the organisation, when they passed each other on the moonlight beach at Cassin.

Three of the passengers on this boat were women, Mary Herbert ('Claudine'), Marie-Thérèse Le Chêne ('Adele') and Odette Sansom, nee Brailly, later Churchill, today Hallowes ('Lise'). For all three there was romance. Madame Le Chêne had come out to be with her husband, H.O. Le Chêne ('Paul'), the Organiser of a network in Clermont Ferand, as his courier. Miss Mary Herbert went to the Bordeaux region to be Claude de Baissac's courier, and ended as his wife. Odette (Mrs Sansom) was intended to proceed to Auxerre, to establish a safe-house, but Peter Churchill asked London for permission to keep her, as his courier, and she too, was destined later to marry her Organiser (though in this case the marriage was eventually dissolved).

This same month a most alarming thing happened. Marsac, travelling from Marseilles to Paris with one of Girard's briefcases full of lists of members, fell asleep on the train. When he woke, his briefcase was no longer with him.

Whatever the case, the security of the plexus of networks along this coast was obviously weak, from a number of causes. Firstly, there were far too many people in it. Starr's story of the sculptor's house in Antibes is an alarming example of the casual involvement of unnecessary people.

---

make better relations than some with his colleagues

When I talked in 1955 with Madame Fourcade (Marie-Madeleine Méric), former head of 'Alliance', she made the point that a clandestine network was not like an army, 'where strength corresponds to numbers. For a clandestine network, one must get into the head that two are weaker than one, three are weaker than two, four are weaker than three... Each one that you take on is an additional security risk, an additional person who can betray you all.' She gave an example. If, amongst the employees of a railway station, one had found one who was so placed as to be able to do useful work for one, and after careful vetting one had recruited him, it was not heartening but really vexatious when, despite one's warnings, he proudly announced he had recruited six others. To make her people understand this was her hardest constant task; it was one, she suggested, SOE never learned. (I have heard Marie-Madeleine's own security placed in doubt, but at least in this she had grasped an essential principle.)

Another reason why the Côte d'Azur complex was insecure was, it was an agglomeration of people who could not stand one another. Quarrels, like love-affairs (other than stable ones) tend to lessen security because they send people rushing about, to see somebody or to avoid seeing somebody, for reasons having nothing to do with the service and in a high state of emotion in which security is forgotten.

Eventually, there took place the great Girard/Frager quarrel, which flared up over the question of who should take the blame for the failure of an attempt to land an aircraft. The quarrel rent the *Carte* network and really brought about its end. Frager, who had been Girard's second in command, left for the Savoy Alps, taking with him Roger Bardet, as his own virtual second-in-command. With him went Peter Churchill, taking Odette and Adolphe Rabinovitch. In retrospect, this can be seen as Peter Churchill's greatest mistake; whatever the inconvenience of working with Girard, with whom he was by this time quarrelling heavily, it could never have entangled him and Odette in the degree of trouble which came from their going with Frager and Bardet.

Girard left for London on October 20, 1942, and was prevented from returning. His broadcasting service in London, headed by Claude Dauphin, was causing annoyance to de Gaulle and to the Free French in London, who found in its transmissions constant barbs against them. It may be that London sacrificed Carte on the altar of peace with de Gaulle. I do not know. (London was already having difficulties through the rivalry of General Giraud to de Gaulle — L'Alliance had strong links with Giraud.)

What I do know is that on May 20, 1955, I received from New York one of the strangest letters which have come to me. It congratulated me on my book *The Starr Affair* (and had been sent to me care of my publisher), and then went on disturbingly. The accusations it made against the direction in London were so appalling that I do not think I can print it in full, but it contained the mysterious statement:

> From higher authorities it was welcomed that the French Resistance could not be too strong at the end — even at the cost of many lives.

It was signed André Girard. The great Carte.

I showed the letter to Starr, to whom he sent his kindest regards. Starr was touched, but could not make it out either. I replied to Girard, asking him if he could explain. This he promised to do when he could visit Europe; it was too dangerous to put on paper. He kept in touch with me for years, sending me each Christmas a hand-painted Christmas card and other examples of his work. He was always coming; he never came. The last communication I had from Nyack was from his widow, to say he had died of a heart attack. And so I still do not know what he had on his mind.

All, finally, that I know of Girard is that he made exquisite paintings: I look at misty gem-like landscapes in tempora, in which the high buildings of New York, with their lights, in an early evening sky have something the quality of Whistler's Battersea Bridge; of memories of Venice in which the dominants are soft turquoise and flame, mist and light; at a large-format art book, the poems of Lucienne Laurentie, a survivor of Ravensbruck (where Girard's wife was), *O Terre de Détresse*, illustrated by himself with grim black-and-whites of figures in the striped camp clothing, with shrunken faces beneath a grey sky, the very ghost of barbed wire.... one of a limited edition of forty copies, the poems hand-written by the artist illustrator; and a small picture unlike the other work he sent me — symbolic — an old man with a red beard lying spread-eagled in the branches of a tree, a phoenix rising from his breast...

The final quarrel between Frager and Girard had taken place on January 2, 1943. After Girard's departure for London, Frager was upset by the thought that in London Girard must be explaining things in his own way. He, therefore, asked to be fetched to London, and on March 23/24 he and Peter Churchill boarded a Lysander. They left behind them, respectively, Roger Bardet and Odette.

The Lysander which took Frager and Peter Churchill away brought Francis Cammaerts ('Roger'). He gave two million francs and a pistol to Marsac and lunched with him next day; the following day Marsac did not come to lunch and in the afternoon Cammaerts learned that he had been arrested. Cammaerts made his way to Annecy. London's idea had been that he would act as lieutenant and liaison officer to Frager, but he did not like the setup. In particular, he mistrusted Roger Bardet (with far better reason than he could know). On the other hand, he did trust Rabinovitch. Deciding for security's sake to cut connection with the people had been supposed to join, he went to a safe-house in Cannes, the address of which Rabinovitch gave him. By this move he almost certainly saved his life; for behind the scenes, Bleicher had entered the picture.

In his post-war statement for the DST, reference SN No. 216/34 p. 782, October 15, 1945, Bleicher states that in March 1943 he was called into the office of Lieutenant-Colonel Reile, chief of Bureau III of the Abwehr, Hotel Lutecia, and instructed to operate with one Kaiser, better known as 'Massuy' (real name Georges Delfanne) and a certain 'Hélène' (believed born Belgian or Dutch) in order to arrest Marsac at a café on the Champs Elysées. After the arrest, he made a number of visits to Marsac in his cell at Fresnes. Marsac told him he had spent the previous night in a hotel, in the bedroom of which would be found crystals (for a radio set) and a million in 1,000 franc banknotes; he asked Bleicher to keep the money and throw the crystals in the Seine. Actually, he says he gave them to his chief, Major Schaeffer.

When he came back to see Marsac he asked him what he wanted of him. 'To get me out of here,' said Marsac. Bleicher replied that if he were to do that, Marsac would have to feign to work for him, and that he must really give some apparent proofs of intent for Bleicher to lay before his chiefs. Marsac reacted against this, saying he could not denounce other agents. It was then that Bleicher spun Marsac the most extraordinary story; he was, he allowed it to be understood, not really hostile to the Allies and would, if he arranged Marsac's escape, have to be collected by the British together with Marsac and taken to London under safe-conduct. Marsac, beguiled, then told him practically all he knew of the organisation; his chief was Frager, at the moment in London, regional chiefs were Castelly, Engel, Elster, Langlois ... he gave the names of perhaps a score of other Resistants; and he wrote a letter for Bleicher to take to Roger Bardet, at Les Tilleuls, St. Jorioz, Lake Annecy, asking him to come with Bleicher to see him in his cell at Fresnes.

Bleicher found at Les Tilleuls not only Roger Bardet and Madame Marsac but Odette; Peter Churchill was still in London. Bleicher was aware Odette was an agent from London, but did nothing about her, for the time being. Bardet he took back with him, to Fresnes; Marsac, holding court in his cell, explained the escape plan to him and Bardet was sent back to St. Jorioz to ask 'Arnaud' (Rabinovitch) to radio London asking for an aircraft to pick up Marsac and a friendly German, 'Colonel Henri', as Sergeant Bleicher was now calling himself. Rabinovitch viewed this approach with the utmost suspicion; but told London of it. The reply which came to him, to share with Odette, was that Colonel Henri was highly dangerous and that they should break contact with him.

Meanwhile, Bleicher had asked Roger Bardet and his girl-friend Mireille Lejeune to meet him, bringing with them two other Resistants, Dujardin and Riquet and Madame Marsac. When they had all arrived, the SD came and placed them under arrest. The same evening, Bleicher, together with Kiki, went to Grenoble to help the Italians make some arrests. He then sent Kiki to Les Tilleuls, pretending to have a message from Marsac; Kiki came back saying more agents were there.

In fact, it was Peter Churchill who had returned from London. His instructions from London were to avoid Odette until he was sure she had eluded Colonel Henri (Bleicher); but she was on the field to meet him when he parachuted and he returned with her to Les Tilleuls, from which she had not departed. Informed by Kiki of the new arrival, Bleicher now moved in with a party and arrested Peter Churchill and Odette that night.

Rabinovitch, more prudent, had removed himself from Bleicher's reach, but fearful lest Peter Churchill should have left compromising papers at Les Tilleuls, at great personal risk, he went in, searched Churchill's room, and in fact retrieved a number of papers which, if the Germans had come back to make the search, would greatly have increased the damage to the Resistance done by that arrest. Having brought out the dangerous papers, Rabinovitch hastened away from the district and made his way back to London, where he made a full report.

Bleicher now visited Roger Bardet in his cell in Fresnes and Bardet immediately offered to work for him; he related to him the entire history of the Carte network from its foundation, and offered, if freed, to resume his contacts in Annecy, Toulouse and the Midi and report on them to the Germans. His release was camouflaged to look like an escape; his former colleagues suspected nothing and from now on Bardet kept Bleicher informed of everything that went on within the great Frager network.

I have in my hand a document, of about 12,000 words, *Le Journal de la Villa Isabelle*. The Baron de Malval showed it to me first in 1955. He had composed it in 1950, with help from the others whose signatures appeared with his at the end, as a protest against the screening in France of the film *Odette*, which they felt to travesty the Resistance, as they had known it. He offered it to me for nothing if I would include it in the book I was then writing, *Double Webs*, but it was not really germane to my subject; later he begged me to print it as an appendix to the paper-back edition and I could not take it. Neither dops it exactly fit in here; and yet I have sympathy with the bitterness felt by himself and his colleagues concerning the enormous concentration of publicity upon two persons, Peter Churchill and Odette, which gave the public at large the false impression that these two were more important than anybody else. Newspaper editors to whom de Malval offered his typescript were frightened to publish it, but in 1958, after years of trying, de Malval was at length able to persuade *The Sunday Dispatch* to publish a few lines from the end of it, calling upon Peter Churchill and Odette to say what effective act of sabotage had been carried out by either of them.

This sudden publication produced a furore, and the fact that the *Dispatch* only printed the two top signatures, Basin and de Malval, created speculation as to the others. Actually, the full list, including those who later joined in, is André Girard ('Carte'), Francis Basin ('Olive'), Henri de Malval ('Antoine'), Marie-Lou Blanc ('Susanne'), Madame E. Experton ('Gisèle'), Henri Coudron, Madame Vautrin (widow of the General), René Casale, Dr Fourest, Madam Détang, Mlle Odette des Garets, Mme Frager (widow), Dr Picaud, the Andouard family and the Stationmaster of la Bocca Railway Station, Cannes. All were people who had belonged to the plexus of networks centred upon Cannes; one could say, it was the Cannes Resistance. The full list can be found printed in articles on the affair which appeared in the French weekly, *L'Express*, of February 29, and *Noir et Blanc* on March 13, 1959. (Exasperation with the publicity surrounding Peter Churchill and Odette had achieved what even war against the Nazis could not, the sinking of differences between Girard and Basin. Girard, having seen a reprint of the *Dispatch* piece in an American paper, had written from the States to de Malval saying he wished to join with them in this, and Basin agreed that Girard's name should go before his own, as recognition that he was 'the big chief'.)

Odette was simply the courier of Peter Churchill, and the mission of Peter Churchill, as Professor Foot has pointed out (Official History, p. 207) was mainly to act as liaison between London and Girard, which, Professor Foot supposes, was why he had no time to carry out any sabotage.

It was not the absence of sabotage, however, which so infuriated de Malval and his fellow Resistants, but the way in which the publicity machine picked out just two people.

Moreover, in the case of de Malval, there was one very personal reason. After his arrest he had been beaten about the head. This was not at Avenue Foch, where his interrogator was 'not too bad — for a Gestapoman'. But at Avenue Foch he had been shown a paper found in the pocket of Peter Churchill when he was arrested; it was a decoded radio-telegramme from London:

ON LANDING IN FRANCE THE SEVEN PASSENGERS WILL PROCEED STRAIGHT TO BARON DE MALVAL VILLA ISABELLE ROUTE DE FREJUS CANNES

De Malval had more than once asked Peter Churchill to destroy this paper, which there was no reason for his preserving. It was not the only incriminating paper kept by Peter Churchill. At one time, Peter Churchill gave de Malval papers, asking him to bury them in his garden. De Malval gave them to Henri Coudron who dug the hole and put them in. About the beginning of February, Peter Churchill had asked for the papers back. After they had been dug up, de Malval looked at them before returning them and was horrified to see that they comprised a journal of Peter Churchill's doings since his arrival, with names and dates of contacts, and comments, some of which were offensive — especially concerning the mystery of Bodington's lost banknotes. For Bodington had hidden beneath dead leaves in de Malval's garden a radio transmitter, documents and 600,000 francs in banknotes. When he went to retrieve his cache, he found the transmitter and the documents but not the 600,000 francs. De Malval was trusted with the funds of the network, which he kept in his safe within the villa. Offence apart, such a journal would compromise everybody should it fall into enemy hands, and de Malval, furious, cut out all names before returning the mutilated pieces to Peter Churchill, telling him that to keep such a diary constituted a great levity.[14] As to the radio-telegramme regarding the arriving passengers, Peter Churchill must have made his trip to London and back again with it still in his pocket.

In Fresnes prison, de Malval passed Peter Churchill, under guard, in a passage, and said to him, 'It's you I have to thank for being here.' Churchill did not answer, but de Malval was sure he heard, because after the war a third person brought him a message from Peter Churchill that it was not he who caused his arrest. De Malval felt that was not adequate. 'I did not mean he did it on purpose, but by his stupidity in keeping that radio-telegramme it was his fault.'

---

14 Even before I met de Malval, I had heard about Peter Churchill's buried narration of his days from Starr, who made the comment, 'He was writing his memoirs during the war!'

He had by this time lost the sight of the eye damaged when he was beaten up after capture.

When the book *Odette* appeared, by Jerrard Tickell (Chapman & Hall, 1949), and he saw reproduced in it what appeared to be extracts from Peter Churchill's diary, he felt sure it was the actual diary which had been buried in the garden of the Villa Isabelle, and that it had been kept, from the beginning, with the intention of using it after the war in a book. He was then absolutely enraged, for it came to him that perhaps the refusal to destroy the radio-telegramme had not been from negligence but from reluctance to part with something which could be put in a book.

What he said to me was that if he had lost his eye in an action undertaken by one of his colleagues against the Germans, even if it had been an action that failed, he would not complain; but he felt, deeply and bitterly, that his eye had been a sacrifice not to the war against the Germans but to Peter Churchill's collection of materials for post-war exploitation.

III: NORTH POLE

'Go to the North Pole with your stories!' This was the rejoinder of Colonel Giskes, German Chief of Military Counter-Espionage (Abwehr) for Holland, Belgium and Northern France, to the NCO who told him an Allied radio transmitter was working from the Hague. Nevertheless, he had the matter investigated and the radio operator captured on March 6, 1942, was Lieutenant H. Lauwers, the first parachuted by SOE Dutch Section. The report made by the NCO was headed *Operation North Pole*. Colonel Giskes could take a joke against himself and adopted this as the official codename of what was to become one of the most remarkable German feats of the war.

Giskes invited Lauwers to resume transmissions to London under German control. What he did not know was that radio operators were told during their training in England that should they be captured they should, after a token resistance, give away their code, but not their security check. This was a spelling mistake which had to appear in a certain square of the grill, individual to each operator. Absence of the security check would tell London the operator was in German hands. Giskes realised there had to be a spelling mistake, but Lauwers was able to persuade him it had always to be made in the punctuation word STOP, irrespective of where it occurred on the grill. To Lauwers' horror, the messages he sent with this improper check were replied to by London as if they were genuine. More agents were parachuted to German reception, on fields convened with London over this circuit.

In this way it came about that all the agents parachuted into Holland were escorted straight to German prisons, and their radio circuits worked back to London. Giskes has detailed the technique in his book *London Calling North Pole* (Kimber, 1953). When he received me at his home in Hamburg in 1955 I noticed, in pride of place in the sitting-room, a large oil-painting of a Dutch landscape with windmill. 'The scene of your former triumphs!' I exclaimed.

'I am very fond of Holland,' he replied. He thought that fondness had little to do with what I had called 'his triumphs'. He had, he explained, been born and brought up in the part of Germany nearest to Holland, where the landscape was much like that of Holland and so were the people. He had grown up bilingual in German and Dutch. Hence, when he was posted to the command in Holland, he had not felt like an enemy imposing himself on a conquered land, and although he realised that most of the Dutch felt more with the English and resented the German occupation, he tried to do his job tactfully because he felt with them, almost as if he had been half Dutch himself.

It struck me, not for the first time, how often those who had played a significant role in these operations had been born by borders, giving them a dual culture and a feeling for both sides, which in some cases gave rise to problems, in others to brilliant successes.

In Giskes's case, I had no doubt that this feeling of being almost one with the Dutch had contributed towards his success. Referring to his having been, at the height of North Pole, composing all the radio messages sent to London in the names of fourteen captured Dutch agents, he said he had feared the sameness of personality transpiring through all the messages would betray their unique origin. 'I said to myself, "They will all sound like me."'

To counteract this, he invented personalities for them. One he made ready to undertake anything, bold even to the point of recklessness; one he made cautious, to a fault; and one he endowed with moral scruples about almost every mission confided to him.

In creating these false personalities, he tried to keep in line with the real personalities of the captured agents, as he sensed them. He spent a good deal of time talking with them. 'I got to know them, imagined them at liberty and tried to react as they would have reacted to the messages coming from London.' He exaggerated the personalities slightly, in order to create something recognisable to London as 'our man'.

If a single agent had been parachuted blind, the whole imposture would have been discovered. But at last London asked one of its agents, Jambroes, code-name 'Anton', to return. This posed a problem for Giskes. He stalled; then, running out of excuses, he agreed. London sent him details of 'three active stations of the British Secret Service in Paris which were working on escape routes' run by French and English personnel with their own radio links with London; Anton was to contact in Paris one 'Marcel', to whom he would make himself known by a password. Giskes said the experienced Belgian guide, 'Arnaud', would conduct him that far. He designated Karl Bodens to play the role of Anton; 'Arnaud' was Giskes's Unteroffizier Richard Christmann.

To me, Giskes confided that during all the years he had Christmann under his command he never knew quite what to make of him. His reports contained a lot of imaginative matter which was vexatious; on the other hand, 'he had a flair for deception work and impersonations,' and so long as no harm to Germany came from Christmann, it seemed to him wise to turn a blind eye to something that was in his opinion 'psychological', rather than to deprive himself of the services of a man who was in some ways a brilliant agent.

I tried to approach Christmann with an open mind, but was later driven to recognise that the warning given me by Giskes concerning his tendency to fabulation was well founded. Nevertheless, the story he told me of his emotionally deprived childhood may explain much.[15]

> Convinced that his second child would be a boy, Richard's father insisted on travelling with his wife from Nancy to Metz through the winter months of 1905, so that his son should be born a German and pursue the military career which he himself had abandoned immediately after having passed out of the Officers' Training College and qualified for a commission, in order to marry the locksmith's daughter, whom his regiment forbade him because he had not the dowry suitable for an officer's wife. While he could not on this account be classed as a deserter, the way in which he left his regiment rendered him liable to some penalty, and it was for this reason he left his country, together with her, for Brussels, where he married her and their first child was born, and later took his family to Spain, whence they returned to France. They came back to her father's home town, in order that their son should take up the father's career as the point where he had left it, and live out his missed destiny as an officer of the Red Dragoons.
>
> So Richard was born at 11.45 in the evening of November 12, 1905, with a problem of nationality built in by circumstance.

---

[15] Christmann to author, at dictation, in French, at Carthage, October 24, 1960. It goes without saying I cannot vouch for the particulars of the narrative.

The hatred between Richard and his father was so great that even today, though his father is dead, he does not feel he has the right to speak of him. His father was disappointed by the sight of what looked to him a weakly baby, which became ill almost as soon as weaned on to cow's milk that had not been sterilised, and developed consequential intestinal troubles which rendered him unattractive. He had continual diarrhoea and wet his bed long after he should have been clean. For his father it was 'not a boy, not a son, nothing.'

His mother loved only her husband and had become accustomed to see everything through his eyes. There was nobody to love Richard. The happiest moments of his childhood were when the maid caressed him or showed him a small kindness; and the first language he learned was French, because it was the maid's language. He did however, enjoy the company of his mother's father, who had a strong sense of nature and taught the children to know the wild creatures in the woods around Metz...

When Richard was thirteen, the Great War came to an end, and Metz was ceded to France. Richard, as a minor, had no nationality until at the age of twenty-one he had to chose either French or German.

He chose German — despite his early leaning to France, though his claim to me to have been awarded the Croix de Guerre with two bars while serving in the French Foreign Legion must, I suspect, be classed with his claim to me that during the North Pole operation a Military Cross was parachuted to him from London, a complete invention.[16]

---

[16] The story Christmann told me about having been awarded a British Military Cross — *Double Webs* (Putnam, 1958), p 152 — is, I am informed by the Foreign Office, 'a complete invention', L.G. Davies, Private Secretary to Anthony Royle, Parliamentary Secretary to the Foreign Office, in a letter to me of April 25, 1973, repeated by Colonel E G Boxshall in letter to me of May 18, 1973

This then was the man, laden with a sense of deprivation, frustrated, ridden by the desire to cut an interesting figure and command attention, whom Giskes now sent into France on a special mission.

IV: PARIS AND THE LOIRE VALLEY, 1942 TO EARLY 1943

By 1943, the drama, in France, had shifted to the Loire Valley. The first SOE agent in the Touraine seems to have been Raymond Flower, alias 'Gaspar' [*sic*], parachuted on June 27, 1942; in civil life a maître d'hotel. He was joined by a radio operator, Marcel Clech, alias 'Georges 60' (in the early period all radio operators of The French Section were called Georges — though there certainly were not 60 of them), who had come from the south, where he had been landed by submarine on the Riviera coast in April. Then came Yvonne Rudellat, alias 'Jacqueline', who had been landed by felucca on the Côte d'Azur in July. Like her chief — for she was supposed to be courier to Flower — she had been in the hotel business, as a receptionist; but they did not get on.

Nearer to the mouth of the Loire, at Angers, another group was establishing itself. E.M. Wilkinson, ('Alexandre') had been parachuted on June 1/2, 1942 together with Cowburn. At Lyons they met Denis Rake, who had arrived by felucca from the south on May 14, then Wilkinson and Rake met Richard Heslop, who had likewise come from the Côte d'Azur, and all three — Rake, Wilkinson and Heslop, were arrested by Vichy police on August 15, 1942. On November 7, when the Germans occupied the hitherto unoccupied zone, the Governor released them, explaining that he would not like them to become prisoners of the Germans, who would probably execute them.

Normally, agents who had been arrested and who had got away, in whatever circumstances, were regarded with great suspicion, as there might be a bad reason for their re-emergence from the land of the dead. In fact, it later became, if it was not then, a rule that any agent who had been arrested, even briefly, should return to London. Rake returned, through the Pyrenees, but Wilkinson and Heslop continued an interrupted journey to Angers. There they made contact with another radio operator, Grover-Williams ('Sebastian') who had since May been working with Robert Benoist ('Lionel') like himself a racing-driver, at the latter's home at Auffargis, to the south-west of Paris. With this radio-link with London, it was arranged that Wilkinson should start a network in Nantes, Heslop in Angers.

This was enterprising, yet one straight away notices the danger-points — the sharing of one radio-operator between several groups, and the possibility Heslop and Wilkinson, having been imprisoned, might have been watched by the police. They seem to have had no doubts whatsoever that it was on purely humanitarian grounds the Governor released them, and one would not like to challenge that; though it is striking that a Governor who released prisoners the Germans wanted to lay their hands on would be likely to be made to suffer for it by the Germans. But however clean the Governor was, men who had spent three months in prison must have been seen by a certain number of persons in the police and prison services, and there must always remain the possibility of their being re-identified.

These were to become not exactly the foundations of the *Prosper* network but they were what was there already when he came.

On the night of September 24/25, two women were parachuted, the first to make an operational jump. They were Lise de Baissac ('Odile') destined to Poitiers, where she was to serve with great distinction, and Andrée Borrel ('Denise') who was to be Prosper's courier, going before to pave the way for him.

Gaspar should have been on the field to receive them, but he was not. Instead, there was Pierre Culioli. Culioli had not been sent out by SOE. He was a Frenchman who had been invalided out of POW camp on December 25, 1940. On return to his native Sologne, he started a small Resistance movement on his own. When Flower (Gaspar) arrived, he met Culioli, and there began a collaboration or rather rivalry. It was the old story, of the man from London with a formal mission versus the native Resistant, who had constituted himself in the area already. One saw it between Olive (Basin) and Carte (Girard).

The two girls asked why Gaspar was not there, and nobody could tell them. Culioli did all the things Gaspar should have done, to help them.

Jacqueline, who was the courier of Gaspar, transferred her services to Culioli, unofficially. This, of course, increased the bad feeling between Gaspar and Culioli.

On October 1, 1942, Prosper himself dropped, received by Culioli; from now on the strife between Flower and Culioli was mortal. Flower conceived a notion Culioli and Jacqueline were both in league with the Germans. This was, I think there can be no doubt, false. Flower, however, reported Culioli to London by wireless as a traitor, and apparently asked for something to kill him with.

When on November 1, 'Archambaud' was parachuted, to be radio operator to Prosper, he brought with him a packet. The packet was marked *Pour Gaspar*. It was Culioli, not Gaspar

(Flower) who received Archambaud on the field, but he afterwards met Flower and gave him the packet. He was horrified when Flower told him it contained a poison pill for secret administration to Culioli. He put it to Flower that, if he distrusted Culioli, he should ask London to fetch him, so that he would be out of Flower's way and could be examined there, rather than kill him. (And while one knows that SOE did prompt the killing of persons believed to be betraying the Resistance to the Germans [Yeo-Thomas told me once of 'our rat-killer' for RF] this poison pill episode may shock others as it shocks me.)

In the end the whole thing was laid before Prosper, and it was really the first serious matter with which he had to deal on arriving to take up his command; he sent Flower back to England, and confirmed Culioli as the officer in charge of parachute receptions, code-name 'Adolfe', with Jacqueline as his courier.

The real name of Prosper was Francis Alfred Suttill. He had been born in Lille, on March 17, 1910, at 5.30 am, son of a Manchester businessman who had settled there and become chairman of the Chamber of Commerce in Lille, and of a French mother. He had been sent to England for education at Stoneyhurst, after which he returned to France to take a French Law degree at the University of Lille; when war broke out he was in Chambers at Lincoln's Inn and was believed to have a future as an international barrister. He had served in the East Surrey Regiment before being transferred to SOE.

Colonel Buckmaster had a first class opinion of him, and indeed he was received in the field as the unquestioned leader. The impression he gave was that he was a character cut in noble mould, a gentleman; though some found him high-handed.

His radio operator and second in command, Archambaud, was in normal life Gilbert Norman, born at St. Cloud on April 7, 1915, at 6.00 pm, son of Mr Maurice Norman, OBE, President of the British Chamber of Commerce in Paris and member of Josolyne Miles & Co., chartered accountants. Gilbert Norman had been educated first at Suresnes, near Paris, afterwards at Mill Hill, London; he was apprenticed to the same firm as his father, and served with the Durham Light Infantry before being transferred to SOE. As illustrative of a certain tenderness in his character, his father told me that as a boy he set in splints the broken leg of a sparrow. His distress over the poison-pill episode is easy to understand.

Denise, a French girl from a petit bourgeois family in Boulogne-sur-Seine, born November 18, 1919, Socialist in her ideas, seems to have been somewhat tougher. This was not her first Resistance work. For two years before she had worked in the *Pat* escape route, until it became so likely she might be arrested that she herself escaped, through Spain, to England, where she was trained for this mission. She had met Prosper during training — indeed he had mentioned to a Mr Louis Graham that he found her very attractive, so much so that the prospect of working long months with her at his side, once they were in France, to some extent troubled him, in as much as he was a married man, and might find the enforced proximity a strain. She was on the field to meet him.

Otherwise, his first contact was Germaine Tambour, who was to be his letterbox. But Germaine Tambour, in private life Girard's secretary, was a member of the Carte network; admittedly that was still flourishing, but from the moment the new network in the Loire valley, that was to cover Paris and the northern half of France, was given a letter-box in common with *Carte* and the complex of networks along the Côte d'Azur and southern half of France, a disaster to one could not be segregated from the other. Peter Churchill had the address of Germaine Tambour; Odette was supposed to contact Tambour before proceeding to Auxerre. Frager had her address, and almost certainly Marsac and Bardet…. whose treason lay still in the future. Prosper, Archambaud and Denise, were all three remembered by Laure Lebras, a recruit of Mademoiselle Tambour's, as visitors to the home of the Tambour sisters, on the Avenue Suffren. Amps, who had dropped with Prosper, to assist Archambaud was also in touch with Germaine Tambour.

One had here a very dangerous structure, an hour-glass with a narrow neck, through which all the sands in either half could flow into the other. So many agents being in touch with one, she could be betrayed by any of them, and she could betray all of them.

It was the kind of structure one feels would have been avoided by persons of any experience in organising clandestine work.

Two more agents, Trotobas and Bieler, were dropped on November 17, 1942, to work in the St. Quentin and Lille areas, and the former, at any rate, had been given contacts with *Carte*, and hence with Frager and Bardet.[17]

The following night brought J.F.A. Antelme ('Antoine'), an agent with an important political mission, to a reception in the Loire valley, and we shall find that he remains in contact with the *Prosper* network.

That Prosper's own security was not above reproach is indicated by an alarming story told me by Armel Guerne, that it was in a nightclub in Montmartre that in December 1942 Prosper and Denise were demonstrating the use of sten guns when he first saw them. Enthusiastic, he was taken on, and

---

[17] *Death Be Not Proud*, Elizabeth Nicholas (Cresset, 1958)

became Prosper's aide, with the code-name of 'Gaspard' — not to be confused with 'Gaspar', and note how confusing these code-names are.

At the end of the year, a new radio operator was dropped, Jack Agazarian ('Marcel'). Agazarian (his curious name comes from his being pure Armenian) was later to boast he had transmitted for twenty-four different networks.

Insecurity was inherent in the build-up.

On the night of January 22/23, 1943, two Frenchmen were parachuted, blind, on to a field near Prithivier, in the Loiret, Henri Déricourt ('Gilbert') and Jean Worms ('Robin').

Worms was to be Organiser of a sabotage network, *Juggler*, in the Marne district, south-east of Paris. Before leaving to be trained in London, he had worked in collaboration with a Swiss, Jacques Weil.[18] Both were Jewish businessmen, Worms small and slight, dark as a gipsy, Weil blue eyed and capable of passing as an Aryan. This he had done so successfully as to make social contacts amongst the Germans to exploit for information. Now that the friends rejoined forces, Worms, having been through the SOE training schools and received a rank, was an official SOE agent, Weil not. Probably it was another of those awkward situations in which the man from London was supposed to liaise with, and practically take over from, the local self-constituted man. But surely there were dangers for an SOE Organiser in associating with a man who had numerous contacts amongst the Germans. Moreover, though it was never mentioned by Weil, Weil had been in the

---

[18] *Pin-stripe Saboteur*, Charles Wighton (Odhams, 1959) inverts the roles, making Weil into Robin the commander of JUGGLER and Worms, the real commander Robin into "Jules"

Interallié.[19] A survivor from the *Cat* disaster on the fringe of the *Prosper* network, could bring Germans in his wake.

Déricourt was to emerge from the war as one of its most controversial figures. A pilot, he had before the war flown for a French civil air line; in September 1942 he left France by the *Pat* escape line, intending to offer his services to the RAF. On its recruiting premises, however, he met Andri Simon, an Air Force officer who had been recruited into SOE. Andri Simon was a conducting officer; that is to say his function was to accompany trainee agents from one SOE training school to another, so that they should not lose sense of continuity when transferred from school to school for the different courses, which were held in different localities. He suggested to Déricourt that he would be more valuable in SOE. Déricourt did not go through the usual series of training schools but was given a special course, at Tempsford, with the RAF, on handling Lysanders, the small aircraft used for landing agents in enemy occupied territory. He was then parachuted back into France as Air Movements Officer, with the task of choosing and laying out fields on which these aircraft could land, receiving agents who arrived by them, and boarding on them agents whom London wished to bring home, as well as any mail.

On January 23, the day that he parachuted, he called on Julienne Aisner, wife of a friend of his, and recruited her to be his courier, and three days later, on January 26, in Marseilles, he recruited Rémy Clément, a pilot whom he had known at Le Bourget, to help him in his duties. These two, who formed his team, were later to receive from SOE the code-names 'Claire'

---

[19] This I have from Elizabeth Nicholas, who obtained a copy of the roll of the Interallié and was startled to see Jacques Weil on it, with code-name 'Atin'.

and 'Marc'. Déricourt rejoined his wife, in their Paris flat, where he resumed living under his civic identity. Resistance without the knowledge of the spouse was practically an impossibility; Déricourt's and Marc's wives were in the know, as were Claire's close associates. Together they would have made a compact team, able to keep themselves to themselves, but that they were obliged to share a radio operator, Agazarian, with Prosper. Both felt very bitterly about this, and Marc may be right in his belief today that none of their troubles need have occurred had Déricourt not been obliged to go for a radio operator to a network which was soon German penetrated from several sides.

Déricourt introduced Worms to a restaurant in the rue Troyon, familiarly known as Chez Tutulle. The next time he went there he saw Worms, Prosper, Archambaud and Denise. After that, he went there no more himself. To congregate in such numbers was folly, for it ensured that if one was noticed by the Gestapo that one could be followed to a meeting with the others, who could all be arrested together.

Déricourt was not, however, sure if I was right in my belief that Denise was the girl-friend of Archambaud in quite the way I thought. It was Madame Balachowsky, who knew the Prosper team well, who had described Denise to me as *'l'amie d'Archambaud'*. Déricourt said she spent days out of Paris with Archambaud, but she also spent days out of Paris with Prosper. They did not appear to quarrel about this and he thought there was an understanding. The British officers preferred to keep to a girl who had dropped from the skies with them than to venture relationship with a local girl who might betray them to the Gestapo. That led to in-turned situations. As I have mentioned on an earlier page, Mr Louis Lee Graham, who had known Prosper in England, told me

Prosper had confided in him before he was parachuted that he was disturbed his courier should be Denise, whom he found most attractive; he was married and would not wish to become unfaithful to his wife but feared he would find obligatory close association with Denise placed a great strain upon his self-control. Elizabeth Nicholas gathered from the sister of Denise, Madame Arend, that Denise was *'un garçon manqué,'* not interested in men.

Nevertheless, a sub-agent of the *Prosper* network with whom I spoke in Paris, told me of an occasion when Prosper and Archambaud quarrelled over Denise during dinner at a small restaurant outside Paris. He intervened to separate and quieten them, lest their raised voices attract the interest of other diners. It was bad for security.

I remember an occasion when, on April 18, 1950, I took coffee at the Café Kleber with John Starr and two officers from the DST, Mangin, the second in command of Wybot, and Inspector Coupaye. The latter said, 'Only the English could have sent their agents out in teams of three, consisting of two men and a girl, without taking account of the fact that it raised a question of which should be the friend of the girl.'

The first air operation organised by Déricourt was on the night of March 17/18, from near Poitiers. Lejeune, Dowlen, Goldsmith and Madame Agazarian, landed and proceeded to useful missions; those leaving included Flower, whose functions as receiver of parachute operations had been taken over by Culioli. Déricourt received only aircraft that landed, not parachutes.

On April 22,[20] Germaine Tambour was arrested, with her sister.

---

[20] I take this date from Laure Lebras, a sub-agent of the *Prosper* network, recruited by Germaine Tambour, who told me the sisters

This was a serious matter for the *Prosper* network, as she was informed concerning so many people. Almost certainly, the arrest of the Tambour sisters was the result of the Marsac/Bardet cave-in.

London ordered that an attempt be made to rescue the Tambour sisters. This may have been in order to prevent their giving away the *Prosper* network under pressure, yet the attempt to recover them from the Germans compromised the *Prosper* network further. Prosper appealed to Jacques Weil, who arranged with an Abwehr man that for a payment of 125,000 francs the sisters would be brought out of Fresnes on some pretext, and released to them at a rendezvous near the Château de Vincennes. The money was paid over, but the women put down from the car were two prostitutes.

Was the mistake genuine, or was it mockery?

Negotiations were renewed, again through the Swiss, Jacques Weil, and an even vaster sum, said to have been 2,000,000 francs, agreed; but this time he cut the notes down the middle, handed over half and promised the remainder after the Tambour sisters had been delivered.

The place was to be near the Porte Maillot. Prosper and Archambaud, waiting to receive the sisters sat at a café from which they could view the spot. This time when the Black Maria drove up and its doors opened, a party of SS men leaped out and Prosper and Archambaud had only just time to get away.

Madame Balachowsky was waiting at the flat of Dr Helmer (a woman) to receive the sisters if the rescue was successful; Prosper and Archambaud arrived, distraught, without the Tambour sisters, and telling her of the SS men who had

---

were arrested on a Thursday which was the eve of Good Friday, 1943.

descended from the van, said, 'We are lost. They photographed us.'

One asks oneself why it was necessary for Prosper and Archambaud to go themselves to this perilous rendezvous; the Swiss did not know the Tambour sisters by sight, but there were lesser members of the network who did. To expose themselves rather than subordinates to the risk of capture may appear heroic, but the chief of a great secret Resistance organisation has not the right unnecessarily to risk himself, because, if he is captured, he has information about so many more whom he might be forced to give away. The probable reason for the insistence of London on the attempts to rescue the Tambour sisters was precisely to prevent their giving *Prosper* away. The Tambour sisters were not rescued.

Meanwhile, Déricourt had conducted two more operations.

It was on the night of April 14/15 on a field at Pocé-sur-Cisse, near Amboise, that an accident occurred. According to what Déricourt told me in 1957 and Marc told me in 1973, the pilot did not put on his landing-light and on touching down taxied into a tree. They walked up and told him he should have put on his landing-light. The pilot, a young one called McCairns, retorted that the ground-light nearest the tree should not have been placed so near to it as to mislead him into supposing he had adequate space in which to land; he had not put on his landing-light because this was enemy occupied territory and he did not want to attract the Germans or anyone who could give them away. They answered him that anybody near enough to see the landing-light would be able to see the aeroplane, too, and hear it; and that if he had put on his landing-light he would have seen the tree. There was obvious damage to the aircraft, which was examined by McCairns, Déricourt and Marc.

Meanwhile, four passengers, Frager, H. Dubois ('Hercule'), P. Liewer and J. Dieudonnet were getting out, while Marcel Clech and three others were boarding. McCairns, Déricourt and Marc agreed after completing their inspection that it would be possible to fly the aircraft back to England, and it took off with its homebound passengers.

Déricourt cycled with the arrivals some twenty miles to Tours, and left them at a school, the headmistress of which, Madame Menon, was the mother-in-law of Dubois. At breakfast time, some Germans arrived. They did not arrest anybody, and according to Dieudonnet they were merely a commission visiting school libraries to make sure that the books were of the 'right sort'. Frager, however, associated their visit, probably wrongly, with Déricourt, and took against Déricourt from this time forth. Ironically, Frager now rejoined Bardet, by this time a German agent.

On the following night, April 15/16, Déricourt received another Lysander, this time at the Pont-de-Braye field, near Vendôme. One of those whom he boarded on this aircraft was Julienne Aisner, later to be called Claire. Déricourt was sending her to England so that she might receive training and make her return as an agent registered in her own right. There was an immense difference in status between the locally recruited sub-agents and the agents who came from London with officer's rank. That Déricourt should have sent for training in London and formal incorporation in the service a person whom he respected, has always seemed to me the guarantee that at least until this time there was no cynicism in his attitude to SOE and he was not playing double.

Meanwhile, the aircraft damaged on the previous evening had returned to England. A French pilot, Roger Herissé, visiting England soon after, was surprised on entering the pilots' mess at Tempsford to see a propeller, detached from its aircraft, propped against the wall, its centre bashed in. Asking how that could have happened, he was told by McCairns that it was 'the fault of the chief of operations', meaning Déricourt's fault.

I spoke in September 1974, with Group-Captain Hugh Verity, who was in command of the pick-up operations. He said a Lysander left Tempsford intact and came back heavily damaged and with a great many twigs and leaves adhering. He received differing accounts of how it came to be involved with a tree. To have brought it back, in such condition, was a feat of skill, and after he had examined it, the list he made out of damaged parts requiring replacement was a long one.

He thought perhaps Déricourt was becoming over-confident, and had an aircraft sent on the night of April 22/23 to fetch him to England for a talk about what had happened. This was not a scolding; the atmosphere was on the contrary very friendly. 'We dressed him up in RAF uniform.' Déricourt appeared pleased and proud. In fact, it was during this period that he was officially commissioned, as Pilot Officer.

I assured Verity Déricourt had not told me it was at Tempsford he felt anything wrong in the atmosphere, but at Baker Street. 'He did go up to London during that period, didn't he? While he was in England over Easter, 1943?'

'I believe that he did.'

The time that he spent in London was pivotal. What happened exactly will perhaps never be known. What is certain is that when he returned to France he was no longer single in heart, and he told me it was during the days he was in London, over Easter, 1943, that he ceased to be so.

Before the war, Déricourt had known Boemelburg. It had come about, he told me, because he and Boemelburg's son were accustomed to attend aerobatic displays and would go with others for a drink afterwards. The young Boemelburg took some of his friends back to his parents' villa at Neuilly; Boemelburg was at that time in Paris as an attaché at the German Embassy. What Déricourt said to me was that he came to England in good faith, and declared his contacts with German intelligence on his arrival (this was confirmed by Lord Lansdowne to Dame Irene Ward[21] at the Foreign Office on December 4, 1958) but that he had been very much shaken during his first weeks in the field by the evident insecurity of the network and what were to him sure signs the Germans could close down on it when they would, and that during the days he spent in London at Easter 1943 he was very disagreeably impressed and thought the direction was indifferent to the agents, indeed that it knew about the German penetration and was allowing it to go on, in the interest of some plan undisclosed to them — that they were sacrificial pawns.

He wanted to get back to France because it was his home and his wife was there, but did not want to be arrested by the Germans when the blow fell, as he felt it must. So he conceived the idea of doing a deal with Boemelburg, which would allow him to carry on his mission for SOE under the surest umbrella.

Obviously, the possibility has to be faced that he was sent by Boemelburg as a spy in the first place, and I suggested this to him, yet the feel of his personality is against this. Though his loyalties were personal rather than national, his feelings were basically pro-Allied; he felt for the French first — particularly what he called 'the small people of France' — and the English second. The few people in England who claimed his respect

---

[21] Today Baroness Ward

were the good people. My feeling about this is that though he was deeply disaffected, with regard to Baker Street, his idea was, by using his wits and talent for establishing a *quid pro quo*, to arrange something in an artful way with Boemelberg which would protect himself and his wife, Marc and Marc's wife, Claire and her friends from arrest without causing arrests; he was trading information concerning the operations for the assurance they would not be hindered. This meant that the safety of agents leaving France by his aircraft was assured, but placed in jeopardy those arriving. He counted, however, upon the Germans' being content to watch these from the shadows, not to arrest them, as by bringing him into discredit with London they would be killing the goose that laid the golden egg. He found the money interesting, but he was not a cold person and I do not believe he would have sent men to a certainty of arrest deliberately.

His return by parachute was on May 5, and he told me he went to Boemelburg within a week of that.

On May 13 Prosper went to London for consultations. Déricourt met him in Paris beforehand, to tell him the date of the flight and the railway station to which he should take his ticket. Then he and Marc met him at Amboise and boarded him on the field near Azay-sur-Cher. Marc maintains that it was on this flight they boarded Madame Gouin, the statesman's wife, whom Déricourt had brought from a nursing-home at Arles, where she had undergone a serious operation.

The same aircraft brought in Claire, on her return from training in England, now possessed of a FANY rank and her own codename. She was now an agent in her own right, no longer a subagent of Déricourt. He nevertheless continued to feel for her, as for Marc, a personal responsibility because it was he who had brought them into SOE. For obvious reasons, however, he had to conceal from them that he was now acting in liaison with the Germans; but he knew — which they did not — that his accord with Boemelburg protected them from arrest. They were under his umbrella.

But the aircraft of May 13 brought in not only Claire but a new team, consisting of 'Elie' (Sidney Jones), Organiser, 'Bastien' (Marcel Clech), radio operator and 'Simone' (Vera Leigh), courier. Though this was new as a team, neither of the men was new in the field. Clech had been landed from the Mediterranean in April 1942 and had, like or with Flower, worked around Tours in the Loire Valley. He had gone back on the aircraft that brought Frager, and was now returning to a district where he was known already. Sidney Jones had also been landed on the Côte d'Azur, by felucca, in late September 1942, and had gone back by the aircraft that took Girard (Carte) and Vautrin in February, 1943. That is to say, they both had past connections with troubled networks, of doubtful security. Now they, and their courier, were to land into a web, or rather into two webs, of deceptions. For the mission of Elie (Jones) was to act as liaison to Frager, in one of those too familiar, awkward relations, in which the London man was to try to take over from the independent man on the spot, and Frager had for his second in command Roger Bardet, who had been, since he fell into Bleicher's hands in March, a German tool.

Between Déricourt and Bardet there was a mortal enmity. The German services, Abwehr and SD, existed always more or less in a state of rivalry with one another and therefore tended to promote their own agents at the expense of each other's. Just when and how Déricourt and Bardet came to know or suspect that each was in relation with a German service — the other German service — I do not know, but by the time the Elie team arrived, Déricourt was actively engaged in trying to trap Bardet so that he would discredit himself with London and be eliminated from the game.

Though Déricourt warned Elie against Frager and Bardet, Bardet was able to persuade Elie and Simone to give him photographs of themselves, on the pretext that he needed them in order to procure for them identity-cards better than the fakes with which they came from London. Bardet gave the photographs to Bleicher, and was indeed able shortly afterwards to provide Elie, Bastien and Simone with first class identity cards, made out for them by the Abwehr. The Elie team never had a chance.[22]

---

[22] In his deposition for the DST, Bleicher gives the names of Elie and Simone correctly, but by the time he came to write his post-war memoirs his memory had slipped In *Colonel Henri's Story*, Hugo Bleicher, translated and edited Ian Colvin (Kimber, 1954) pp 111-14, he calls Elie Ellis and Simone Denise, creating confusion with the *Prosper* network

V: THE TERRIBLE JUNE

We left Colonel Giskes sending Christmann and Bodens to Paris, Bodens to impersonate the Dutch agent Anton, whom London wanted back, and Christmann to present himself to the Resistants as the Belgian guide, Arnaud. They were to meet Marcel, to whom they would identify themselves by exchange of passwords, at an address arranged with London over the radio and make themselves known to them by a password radioed from London. Before they went to this rendezvous they were, however, to call at the HQ of the Abwehr in Paris, at the Hotel Lutecia, and ask them to stage the mock arrest of Anton in sight of the Resistants, just before he was supposed to leave with them for Spain, so that London would receive from the Resistance an explanation of his failure to return.

In view of Giskes's understanding of how the operation was to proceed, the glimpses we have of what happened are mystifying.

At dusk on the evening of Thursday, May 20, 1943, a blond stranger called at the restaurant in the rue Troyon known as Chez Tutulle, and asked for 'Gilbert'.

The proprietors, Monsieur and Madame Touret, supposed he meant Archambaud, that is Gilbert Norman, whom they knew only under his cover-name of 'Gilbert Aubin'. The difference between agents, who knew the code-names, and unregistered sub-agents such as the Tourets is important. The Tourets acted as a letterbox, with whom members of the team could leave messages for one another, but for them Gilbert was the dark young man who came in for lunch as part of the usual group.

Thinking to be helpful, they therefore told the stranger that Gilbert came in to lunch almost every day, but that if it was urgent, he could be found playing poker at the flat of the Bussoz family, 10 Square Clignancourt, close to the extreme northern perimeter of the city of Paris.

The stranger was Christmann.

What happened next is obscurely tangled. Christmann was closely interrogated about this after the war by the French authorities, in 1946, and also, informally, by me, in Frankfurt in 1955 and in Carthage in 1960. Each time he has told the story he has given details differently, and the only certainty is that he did arrive that evening, with or without Bodens (Bodens denies having been inside the flat, but Agazarian's deposition mentions two Resistants from Holland), and encountered Archambaud (Gilbert Norman), Denise, Agazarian, Marcel Charbonnier, Alain Bussoz and an unidentified woman, and said they needed Gilbert's assistance to arrange a Lysander passage to England; Archambaud said one of his names was Gilbert but he was not the Gilbert who arranged Lysander passages, and an arrangement was made to meet at the Capucines Restaurant, at which it was hoped Gilbert-Lysander (Déricourt) would be present.

That night, Agazarian came to tell Déricourt, but Déricourt did not like the sound of it and declined to go with Agazarian to the rendezvous with the Dutchman (he said he was only told there was one Dutchman) at the Capucines Restaurant.

It will be noticed that the meeting with the Resistants did not in fact take place at a rendezvous pre-arranged with London over the North Pole radio so that their Dutchman could be inserted into an escape-line for Spain; Christmann picked up at a restaurant the address at which he could find somebody he had heard of called Gilbert, whom he hoped was the Gilbert who sent people by air to England.

There has been difference of testimony as to the date of the meeting at the Capucines, but I have no real doubt that it was Wednesday, June 9. Agazarian was present, and Bodens, and it is not clear how many of the others. The SD entered and arrested Bodens. Agazarian went, very agitated, to tell Déricourt, and also informed London. Just after this Christmann was at SD HQ, 84 Avenue Foch, talking to one Gutgesell 'to explain'; just what he had to explain is unclear, for his statement varies every time, but obviously he would have felt obliged to go and explain that Bodens was, like himself, German; and so extract him.

One sees that nothing had gone according to Colonel Giskes's plan; Christmann and Bodens had not gone to the Abwehr HQ, and the arrest of Bodens was not the mock arrest by the Abwehr which Giskes had instructed them to have laid on. It was an arrest by the SD, which gave Christmann and Bodens a great fright.

As Déricourt pointed out to me, only one of those who knew of the meeting to take place at the Capucines Restaurant could have betrayed it to the SD, and he gave me the broadest possible hint that it was he, himself, who did so. What I think happened is this: he did not want the Germans to arrest his friend and colleague, Agazarian, but he suggested to Boemelburg the arrest of Bodens, simply to give him a fright and make him go away, as an Abwehr intrusion would over-complicate a situation already delicately balanced.

As to why the plan as conceived by Colonel Giskes was departed from by his subordinates, without their ever informing him, a possible motivation suggests itself flagrantly. Christmann has never said outright, yet more than once his words to me have seemed to drop an oblique clue: he toyed with the idea of going, himself, to England, to hold conversations with his London contact regarding his gem-smuggling operations, he said. It could have been to do something else.

But what about the radio communications between Colonel Giskes and London in the course of which 'Marcel' was mentioned? Marcel was the code-name of Agazarian. If Marcel was really mentioned in the transmissions from London received by North Pole, as Huntermann, chief of Giskes's radio department averred, then it could only have been Agazarian who was the subject of reference. But as the country sections in London were not in touch, how would the Dutch Section have heard of a French Section agent? I have been in touch with the Foreign Office about this, but Colonel Boxshall's replies make it plain that they have no records that would shed light on the matter — the SOE records were weeded at the end of the war before being passed to the Foreign Office for storage — and that it was 'a problem that has so far defied any solution'.

I notice that Professor Foot says, in the official history, p. 309, that 'Jacques Agazarian (Marcel)... claimed to have transmitted for no fewer than twenty-four different agents.' He was an eager enthusiast who ignored admonitions that he should transmit only for those to whom he was officially attached. It seems to me possible that, although the country sections and Escapes section were not supposed to enter into contact — but we know that they did, as de Vomécourt and Turck — Agazarian had come to be transmitting for an escape line, to which the Dutch Section in London would have had to have recourse once it decided upon instructing one of its agents to come back, through Spain. There is a difficulty to this solution, too, that if by chance they met at Square Clignancourt the contact London had intended, Agazarian would have made some comment about this; and yet I cannot see any other explanation which allows for all the discordant but definite facts.

The happening at the Capucines brings us into the terrible June of 1943. Before looking at some of the other threads which led to the cataclysm, let us finish with Christmann's intervention. The Abbé Guillaume sent me an extract from a deposition by Marcel Charbonnier in which he said a few days after the encounter at Square Clignancourt, on the orders of Gilbert-Archambaud he met the 'Dutchman' in the Pigalle district, and gave him a radio-set.

The 'Dutchman', here, must be Christmann, as Bodens could not speak a word of French. But what use did Christmann make of an SOE wireless-set? That is a question which has not been answered. What one sees, however, is Christmann working himself further into the *Prosper* network.

In one of his letters to me (September 29, 1955), Christmann wrote:

> I can affirm Marcel, who arranged the rendezvous of Alain, Bodens and myself at the café, was conducting a black-market in gold and diamonds in 1943. We made a report to London about the various traffickings of Marcel, so as to get Marcel put aside by London. I believe, moreover, that Marcel was punished by London following our report.

At the time, I took the references to be to Marcel Charbonnier, for I did not then know the code-name of Agazarian was Marcel. Re-reading this old letter today, it is abundantly clear to me that the subject of Christmann's reference was Agazarian.

As with all Christmann's statements, there is the need for a reserved judgement. I would hesitate categorically to assert that a dead man trafficked in gold and diamonds on Christmann's evidence. Yet I cannot see a reason for his having made this up. What I doubt more is whether he made a 'report to London', which sounds too grand. Christmann was not a radio-operator, and over what circuit would he have transmitted? Possibly he spoke a few words in the ear of Archambaud, if he wanted Agazarian out of the way. But from what point of view was Agazarian in Christmann's way? Did he want to take his place in a smuggling ring or in his service capacity?

At my second meeting with Christmann, in Carthage in 1960, I dropped a reference to Weil. He asked like a flash, 'Weil of the all-Jewish network? You know that there was one network of the French Section which was all Jews?'

I recognised at once a reference to the *Robin* network. Worms, Weil, Cohen and Sonia Olschanewsky were all Jews. Whether there was any truth in the story Christmann told me about Weil I cannot know; but what was plain to me from his rapier-quick reaction was that Christmann knew all about that network, which probably meant that he had met at least one or more of its members.

These are all loose ends, which I have not been able to follow to their conclusion; but which are significant in themselves in as much as they all of them show Christmann worming his way through the Paris-based networks of SOE.

In addition, Denise lodged at 51 rue des Petits Ecuries, over a café frequented by French agents of the Avenue Foch, Mario

Bay and Michel Bouillon, who according to her landlord watched her movements.

There is also the fact that on two occasions, in May, German soldiers had come to the house at Triechâteau, near Gisors, belonging to a Madame Guépin, where Prosper and Archambaud stayed, when in Normandy; on one occasion when they were there, although apparently bluffed, the soldiers may have reported suspicious activity at the house.

Wilkinson had by now been arrested. It will be remembered he and Heslop had been released by the Vichy police and had established themselves in Nantes and Angers, respectively. Now Imar, one of the Vichy inspectors who had participated in their interrogation while they were prisoners appealed to Wilkinson (how did he know how to contact him unless he had had them shadowed?) on behalf of two other agents. Against advice, Wilkinson went to the offered rendezvous, in a café, and was arrested, on June 6,[23] three days before the Capucines charade.

Hitherto, we have followed, in France, mainly the entanglements of Colonel Buckmaster's French section. But République Française, the de Gaulle Section, was by now riding for its own crisis in the terrible June. The head of its military *armée secrète* in France was General Delestraint. On May 29 he had seen a colleague, Henry Aubry, who had just become his chief of staff, following the arrest of the former one, Morin-Forestier, and told him he wanted to know the reply of René Hardy, to whom he had offered the post of chief of his Troisième Bureau. He would be at the Metro station Muette at 9 am on June 9, and left to Aubry the pains of telling Hardy to be there. Aubry delegated the passing of the message to his secretary, writing it out in clear for her to carry but not,

---

[23] *Xavier*, Richard Heslop (Hart-Davis, 1970), p 137

apparently, telling her where she was to take it, and without thinking to warn her that a certain letterbox, *chez* a Madame Dumoulin, was now known to the Germans. She took it there. (There has been a certain amount of contradictory witness about this episode, but I feel, with Noguères, that one can accept the resumé by Maurice Garçon, counsel for Hardy at his eventual trial, of what emerged from the evidence of those involved at this point.)

In fact, Hardy knew that that letterbox was suspect and had reported it to his colleagues — that seems to be uncontested — therefore he did not go to it, did not receive the message and did not know he had been summoned to a meeting with General Delestraint at 9 am on June 9 at the Metro Muette.

The message was picked up by a double-agent named Multon, alias 'Lunel'. Multon had been arrested in Marseilles on April 27, by Dunker, chief of the SD of Marseilles, and 'turned' by him. From May 24, Multon had been lent by Dunker to Klaus Barbie, chief of the SD of Lyon, a man of the most brutal repute. Barbie made Multon responsible for the surveillance of the Dumoulin letterbox, from which he learned that one 'Didot' was summoned to the Metro Muette ….

It happened that Hardy, although he did not know he was summoned, had another rendezvous in Paris on that date and travelled up by the night train on June 7 or 8. His ticket was bought to him the day before by his courier Bossé, and his sleeping reservation obtained for him by his fiancée, Lydie Bastien; he had bed No. 8 in carriage 3 818. In the adjoining compartment, beds no. 9 and 10 were occupied by Multon and another double agent, Moog. Hardy saw Multon on the platform, and knowing or suspecting him to have been turned, said to a colleague, Racheline, 'If anything happens to me, tell Benouville it was the fault of Lunel.'

At 1 am, at Châlons-sur-Saône, Hardy was taken off the train and handed over to German police. Up to this point, the story has been relatively simple. What happened during the two or three days Hardy was in German custody has been disputed and argued ever since.

On June 9, at 9 am, General Delestraint arrived on foot at the Metro Muette. A French double agent, Saumandre, met him and told him Hardy thought the situation dangerous and asked him to join him a little further off. Suspecting nothing, Delestraint walked with him, mentioning as they went that in half an hour's time he had an appointment with two other colleagues, Gastaldo and Theobald, at the Metro Pompe. Then he found himself pushed into a car and made prisoner. In the car was Moog. It was driven on to the Metro Pompe, where Gastaldo and Theobald were arrested at 9.30.

It seems Barbie did not go to Châlons-sur-Saône to question Hardy until the following day. He knew his civil identity, for Hardy had his papers on him. What has been questioned is whether he knew Hardy was the 'Didot' whom General Delestraint expected to come to meet him at the Metro Muette. Hardy, at his eventual trial, maintained that Barbie never knew it, and released him because he was finally convinced he had nothing to do with the Resistance. Yet Hardy also said Barbie told him of the arrest of General Delestraint, and that it was that which decided him not to tell his colleagues in the Resistance of his arrest, when he rejoined them, in case they should think it was he who had betrayed General Delestraint and purchased his liberty by so doing.

However that may be, to have concealed his arrest from his colleagues was a grave fault. It was a primary rule that an agent who had been arrested must report it; firstly because of the possibility that he might have been 'turned round', and secondly because, even if he had managed to make an innocent get-away, he might be still under surveillance and so capable, even without intending it, of leading the enemy to his friends.

On June 11 and 12 were arrested General Fèvre, head of the ORA and General Olleris of the ORA. These Generals were nothing to do with de Gaulle's organisation. They represented part of the former Armistice Army which Hitler had allowed Pétain to keep until November 1942. It will be remembered that Girard (Carte) had maintained that a great part of this army, with which he was in contact, was secretly pro-Allied, with Generals capable of forming an army within an army. London (except for Bodington) had treated Girard as a dreamer, a head-in-the-clouds, yet the fact is that, although Girard was kept out of things by hot being allowed to return from his visit to London, a number of the Generals did form themselves into a secret group, calling itself the Organisation de la Resistance de l'Armée (ORA); so perhaps Girard was not such a dreamer, after all. But if ORA was the child to which Carte had tried to be midwife, it was beheaded by the arrests of Generals Fèvre and Olleris on June 11 and 12.

To return to the French Section on the night of June 15/16, two Canadians, 'Bertrand' (Frank Pickersgill) and 'Valentin' (John Macalister) were parachuted into the Loire valley, and were received by Culioli, and they were temporarily lodged near where they had come down.

On the following night, of June 16/17, there was another Déricourt operation, from a field at Le Vieux Briollay, a few miles north of Angers. The passengers leaving included Agazarian (according to Foot [p. 314] this was at the insistence of Prosper, who suspected him of being too careless — which could fit in with Christmann's notion of Agazarian's being 'punished' for something — though Prosper was at the time in London) and Agazarian's wife. The incoming passengers were 'Madeleine' (Noor Inayat Khan), 'Paulette' (Diana Rowden), 'Alice' (Cecily Lefort) and 'Monk' (C. Skepper).

Marc (Rémy Clément) told me that he travelled together with Madeleine in the train from the little station at Ettriché to Paris. It was clear that he found her touching and pathetic, from the way in which he said, *'Elle avait très peur.'*

I do not believe literally in the boast later made by Dr Goetz of the Avenue Foch that he had watched the arrival of Madeleine from the shadows. That was probably said to add to the dismay of a prisoner. Nevertheless, I take it as virtually certain the Germans knew of this operation from Déricourt, even though none of the arrivals were interfered with.

Diana Rowden went to join John Starr, who was now on his second mission, in the Jura, to serve with distinction as his courier.

Skepper went south and became the Organiser of a network in the Marseilles area, which ran for nine months, being rounded up in the end only as the result of a local denunciation.

Cecily Lefort went to serve as courier to Cammaerts in an adjacent district, the Basses Alpes.

Noor Inayat Khan (Madeleine) was to assist Archambaud, as a further radio operator to the *Prosper* network, and we shall hear of her again. Her instructions from London were to go first to an apartment at 40 rue Erlanger, Paris, to see 'Cinema' (E.M. Garry).

Madeleine must after that have met Archambaud, for it was he who conducted her, probably the next day, to the Agricultural School at Grignon, the working headquarters of the *Prosper* network, at which he introduced her to Professor and Madame Balachowsky.

In the small hours of June 20, Prosper was parachuted back and received by Culioli. He travelled straight up to Paris, and later in the morning saw Madame Balachowsky.[24]

> Four days before the arrest of Prosper we all lunched at the school at Grignon. Afterwards I walked with Prosper, who was looking for grounds for gliders, and it was that day I told him I was in contact with Madame Monier-Vinard [a lady who was arranging escapes to England via Gibraltar].... and that if he needed to communicate with London without passing through Gilbert [Archambaud] he could count on me. We talked at length, haunted by Gaspard [Guerne], whom François [Prosper] was trying to get away from all the time. That day I spoke to him of the imprudence of Denise, Gilbert [Archambaud] and Gaspard; he agreed and felt himself very much alone, surrounded by people who were insecure, not by their lack of courage but by their lack of seriousness. I retain, as I have told you, a profound admiration for Prosper, and I think often of that admirable soul, that gentleman .... Prosper supposed there must be a German agent in London...

Later that day, in Paris, on the steps of the Gare Montparnasse, from which she was taking the train to Viroflay, he told her he feared that all their movements were known to the Germans, and had been for some time.

It was the last time she saw him.

That same day the Germans went to Avaray where they asked for '*la mère Michel*', which was the code-name of a Madame Boissard, letterbox shared by Prosper and his network with Frager and Bastien (Clech) of the Elie team. Somebody directed them to a Madame Michel, whom they arrested, but

---

[24] Letter from Madame Balachowsky to author, December 20, 1958

released when they realised she was not '*la mère Michel*'. Frager and Bastien however, were so well known to the Abwehr through Bardet and Bleicher that the real significance of this episode lies in the bridge it makes between the *Frager* and *Prosper* networks. Bastien's every transmission was listened in to and recorded by the Germans, and he transmitted from a villa at Aulnay-sous-Bois rented by the Monsieur Boissard who lived in the house at Avaray where his wife was the letterbox.[25] Thus there was a direct lead to Prosper from this direction.

From about midnight the region of the Sologne around Bracieux, Dhuizon and Neuvy began to fill up with German troops. This was very close to where Culioli lived, at Velleins, and most of the fields on which he received parachute drops were in this area. What brought them? The Abbé Guillaume attaches importance to peculiar explosions which took place on the night of June 13, when containers were being received. Apparently what had happened was that the aircraft, being a bomber, had bombs which it accidentally released at the same time as the containers, and as these contained explosives, intended for the use of the Resistance, the bombs not only exploded themselves but exploded the explosives in the containers. Culioli, Jacqueline and their team, including on this occasion the Comte and Comtesse de Bernard, waiting on the field to receive the containers, were lucky not to have been killed, and a farmer in one of the neighbouring farms, alarmed, called the police, who in their turn informed the German police, who were on the scene in no time, examining the craters.

That would have focussed attention on the district, and Culioli had got Archambaud to send a message to London asking that no more parachute deliveries be made for the time

---

[25] *La Sologne*, Paul Guillaume (Orleans, 1950), pp. 58-59.

being; notwithstanding, the Canadians, Pickersgill and Macalister, were parachuted two nights later. He still had them in his house. On June 17/18 there had been the parachuting of Raynaud, on June 19/20 of Prosper. Perhaps there had just been so much whirring of Allied aircraft in the district that Ludwig Bauer, the commandant of the Gestapo of Blois, for it seems to have been he, had men sent out on the following night.

A Madame Dambrine, who was bold enough to ask one of their officers what they were doing, was answered, 'You have nothing to worry about, Madame. There is a centre of English espionage in this neighbourhood.' And Madame Montprofit, wife of the Major of Dhuison, when they entered her house, said, 'There's nothing hidden here,' and was answered, 'We are not looking for material, we are looking for someone.'

There had in fact, been dropped that night just three consignments of arms, to three of Culioli's teams, on three different fields; at about 6 am a lorry carrying the arms from the field at Villeny was stopped by Germans at Dhuizon and the men on it escorted, with their hands tied behind their backs, to the prison of Blois.

Just afterwards, Culioli's car entered Dhuizon. He was carrying the two Canadians, who he had harboured since the 16. They were supposed to proceed to the Nord, the North of France, there to create a new network, and he was taking them as far as Paris, there to hand them over to Armel Guerne. With them in the car was Jacqueline. They found themselves halted, but then were allowed to pass on, and it was too late to turn back now that they realised that Dhuizon was full of German police. At the second road-block, the two Canadians were made to get out, and replaced by two armed soldiers; Culioli was required to drive to the Mairie. There he and Jacqueline were made to get out and enter. They found themselves amongst a dozen other persons who had been brought in for questioning. 'Why are you out and about at this hour?' he was asked.

He was able to satisfy the questioner, and was, with Jacqueline, allowed to get back into the car. He could, now, have driven off, abandoning the Canadians; but he stayed for them. They came up on foot and were required to enter the Mairie. They must in some way have excited suspicion — Culioli, and Yeo-Thomas (who knew them at Buchenwald) have asserted their French was not good — for Culioli heard a cry from within the Mairie, then the door opened and a German soldier called him and Jacqueline to come back. He put his foot down. Germans jumped into another car and followed, and, as they began to overhaul the Citroen, outside Bracieux, opened fire. At the same time, a detachment at the entrance to Bracieux fired on the advancing car, smashing the windscreen. Jacqueline, badly wounded, fell across her companion. Culioli, thinking to commit suicide, drove the car into a wall, but it cannoned off into a field. He was thrown out, and, as Germans sprang on him and he struggled, he was shot in the leg. He and Jacqueline were then taken back to the Mairie at Dhuizon, where the Canadians were still held.

Culioli was given first-aid treatment, then confronted with what had been found in the car, two radio-sets, crystals for their own circuit and a crystal permitting Archambaud to change his wavelength, the latter wrapped up in a cloth with a label marked in English, 'For Archambaud' and two envelopes marked respectively Prosper and Archambaud, which contained messages.[26]

---

[26] *Op cit*, pp 66-72, and Abbé Guillaume to myself verbally

Prosper went that morning to the Gare d'Austerlitz with Armel Guerne to meet Culioli and the two Canadians, unknowing the fate that had befallen them on the way. With him, Prosper brought Richard Heslop (Xavier) and a young English pilot, Taylor, who had been shot down over France, by good fortune within a few paces of a house belonging to members of the *Prosper* network, who had put him straight into contact with the big chief. Heslop was expected back in London by the next air passage, and Prosper asked Déricourt if he would take the shot-down RAF man under his wing and board him on the same plane. To this, Déricourt assented cheerfully, taking upon himself the responsibility of using the plane sent from London to board a passenger which London had not asked for but should certainly be glad to receive.[27]

He took Heslop and Taylor away, gave them the usual instructions as to the train they must board — from which station and to which station — in two days' time, then parted from them.

Prosper and Guerne, not finding Culioli and the two Canadians come off the train that should have brought them, did not hang about.

The same morning was fatal for the de Gaulle section. Jean Moulin, greatly concerned by the arrest of General Delestraint, head of the Secret Army, was now faced with having to reorganise it. In the first place, a new General would have to be nominated to the command of it, and there were other changes he had in mind to make. A meeting with those whom he must consult had to be convened immediately but because it was a summit meeting, the utmost precautions were taken with

---

[27] Déricourt to myself, verbally and in letter, also *La Sologne*, Abbé Guillaume, p 63 (the latter presumably on Guerne's witness)

regard to its security. Thus, they were not told exactly when or where the meeting was to be. They were told in the first place that it would be round about a certain period, and in or near Lyons. This meant that by the period in question they had to be in Lyons and accessible so that they could be given more precise indications closer to the time, which itself they would not know ... it was rather like that child's game in which someone gets 'warm... warmer...'

During the morning of June 21, all those who were to come were contacted *seriatim* at the different rendezvous they had been given — at various points along the banks of the Rhone and roundabouts — and told to present themselves, at staggered times, at different, though not far distant, places in the neighbourhood of a funicular railway. For instance, one, Aubrac, had to present himself at the top of the funicular at 1 pm, when a guide would appear to him whom he must follow. Another, Aubry, had to be present at 1.45 pm at the bottom of the funicular, when he would be met by one of the organisers, Lassagne, whom he must follow.

When Lassagne met Aubry, he was surprised to find he had René Hardy with him. Aubry had taken the liberty of bringing him along, because he wanted him to sustain him on a point he had been disputing with Jean Moulin. Lassagne, although surprised by the presence of Hardy — whom he knew, although he knew he had not been convoked — gave the further instructions. They were to follow him. He would mount the funicular in the next car. They would mount in the car that followed. Afterwards, they would follow him by No. 33 tram, to the Place Castellane, in Caluires.

One must now mention a woman; Madame Deletraz. She had belonged to the Lyons branch of the *Gilbert* network (nothing to do with either Déricourt or Archambaud) of

Colonel Groussard. After being arrested, she agreed to work for the Gestapo, but kept her former colleagues informed, and became valuable to them in that she could warn them what the Gestapo were planning. On the morning of June 21, very blond, with red corsage, she arrived at the Croix-Rousse where she thought to find an officer of the ORA. On being told he was not there, she told her dreadful news to one of the others present: a few minutes ago, in the office of the Gestapo, 'one named Didot, called Hardy' [*sic*] had come in to announce that a meeting of the chiefs of the Secret Army would take place at about 13 o'clock. He would be there, but did not as yet know the place; they would, however, only need to follow him. She was the one detailed by the Gestapo to follow him.

At Hardy's eventual trial, another witness, Bossé, said that at the time stated by Madame Deletraz, just before mid-day, Hardy was lunching with him. Hardy's counsel, however, did not challenge the evidence of Madame Deletraz, which received a certain amount of corroboration in respect of her endeavours to warn members of the Resistance, but suggested that Barbie, piqued by Hardy's deception of him at Châlons-sur-Saône, deliberately framed him so as to make him appear to the Resistants as a traitor, in order to get him killed by them.

Whatever happened in the office of the Gestapo, the position at the bottom of the funicular at 1.45, was that Lassagne was in the lead, followed by Aubry and Hardy; Madame Deletraz was following Hardy and Aubry, and the Gestapo were following Madame Deletraz. In this manner they mounted the funicular in successive cars and proceeded in a crocodile. Because of the separation between the ORA and the de Gaulle organisation, Madame Deletraz did not know whether her friends had been able to warn those attending this meeting (and in fact they had not), so she led the Gestapo as tardily as possible. After returning to them from the house of a Doctor Dugoujon, which she had seen Aubry and Hardy enter, she managed to take them by a wrong way, pretending to confuse the streets. She achieved, in fact, a delay of three quarters of an hour, arriving with the Gestapo not at 2 pm when the meeting began, but at 2.45. If the meeting had been a prompt and short one, it might by now have been dispersed. Unfortunately, Jean Moulin arrived only just before 2.45.

As he was normally a punctual man, there has been much speculation as to what delayed him, but that is hardly material. The meeting had barely started when Aubry, seated near the window, saw a great number of men in leather jackets approaching. He told the others, 'It's the Gestapo!' Hardy drew his pistol, and was told by the others to put it away. The Gestapomen entered and said, 'hands up!' In no time, everyone had his hands secured behind his back by handcuffs, except for Hardy. When the Gestapomen arrived at him, they had run out of handcuffs. While the prisoners were being led from the house towards waiting vehicles, Hardy ran away, his arm being hit by one of the German bullets which followed him.

At one stroke, the de Gaulle section in France had lost all its heads. Jean Moulin died of the atrocious treatment he received at the hands of the Lyons Gestapo.

It was a rule of the Resistance that if an appointment was missed the party who had kept it did not wait, but both parties held it good for the same time and place on the following day. Guerne recalls that Prosper was not too worried by the failure of Culioli to arrive with the two Canadians at the Gare d'Austerlitz on June 21, as he thought Culioli could have had difficulties with a parachute reception during the night which caused delay. It was therefore with a reasonable expectation that they would turn up that he went to the Gare d'Austerlitz again at the same time on the morning of June 22.

After his vain journey, says Guerne, he came back to Guerne's flat for lunch, at 1 pm.[28] Denise, he says, was also there, but not Archambaud. Guerne told me that Prosper, at that lunch on the 22 was very much agitated and distressed lest the Allied invasion of the continent should not be that summer. Guerne told me, in categoric terms, that Prosper at that lunch affirmed that if there was not an Allied landing he and Archambaud would provoke one, by calling out the whole of their network, which, being the largest of the French Section ones, would bring the others out in its wake, so forcing the hand of the Allied High Command — since an unsupported Resistance would be massacred and useless for later. I asked Madame Balachowsky about this, and she assured me she did not for a moment believe Prosper had spoken so, though she confirmed that Prosper was anxious lest the invasion should not be that summer, as 'we should otherwise all be arrested,' first.

However, Madame Guépin says that on June 22 Prosper, Archambaud, Denise and she had lunch at the Café Triadoux-Haussman, when they discussed reception of a parachute drop expected near Gisors.[29]

Obviously, either Guerne or Madame Guépin is mistaken about the date of the lunch. Probably one of the lunches was on the 23rd, unless one of them is thinking of a dinner.

Madame Guépin was, in any case, very shocked by Prosper's appearance on his return from England. 'I hardly recognised

---

[28] Guerne to author, verbally May 16, 1957, and Guerne, 15 1 49, to the Abbé Guillaume, cited by latter in *La Sologne*, p 73
[29] Deposition of Madame Guépin to French authorities, 4 7 47, and Madame Guépin to author, verbally, November 24, 1955

him, he looked so grey and strained.' On the evening of the 23rd, he went out to Gisors, to talk to some people about the parachute reception, and stayed the night at Madame Guépin's house. She asked him if he was ill, but he replied, 'It's not my health. It's much worse. I have not the right to tell you the trouble which weighs on my mind.'

Marcel Charbonnier, who saw him early the next morning at Gisors, also remarked how uneasy he was, urging strict precautions.

Prosper was catching the 7 am train from Gisors, which should get him into the Gare St. Lazare, Paris at 9 o'clock. Madame Guépin knew that he had an appointment with someone in Paris that morning, though not with whom. She went with him to the station, and felt he had a presentiment it was the last time they would meet. Having said good-bye, he came back twice to say good-bye again.[30]

Between midnight and 0.15 in the morning of June 24, a Monsieur Nicholas Laurent was wakened by ringing at the doorbell. Going down, he opened the door to a young man who asked for '*Gilbert, de la part d'Archambaud.*' Laurent, being only a locally recruited sub-agent of the network, knew his lodger only under his cover-name of Gilbert Aubin. He therefore woke him and gave him the message without knowing that he was Archambaud. Archambaud, evidently taking for granted that anybody who knew his code-name must be a colleague, got out of bed at once and came straight downstairs. Fifteen men jumped on him. Then they went upstairs and arrested Denise, who was spending the night at his lodgings, too; Monsieur and Madame Laurent were also taken away in the police car. They were driven to the Avenue Foch.

---

[30] Madame Guépin to myself, verbally, November 24, 1955

Despite the hour, the lights were on and the whole place in a state of activity as though it were day-time. Culioli was brought up from Blois the same night.

At about 1 am or 1.30 am that morning, the morning of June 24, a number of men in civilian clothes, from the Avenue Foch, arrived at an obscure hotel, the Hotel Mazagran, in the narrow rue Mazagran, in a shabby district near the Porte St. Denis, and asked for Desprée. While the proprietress gaped at them, too frightened to move, they seized the register and saw from it that from June 20 Room 15 had been occupied by François Desprée. Madame Févre said that he had not come in that night, but they took the key and some of them went upstairs, while others waited below with her, perhaps so. that she should not give a warning. Dawn turned to daylight, and still hours passed. She supposed it was midmorning — perhaps between 10 and 11 — when she saw the men coming downstairs with Monsieur Desprée. She had not seen him come in and go up. All left together.[31]

So, Prosper was arrested.

---

[31] Madame Févre to author, verbally, November 26, 1955, and Madame Févre to the DST, cited in *La Sologne, p 76*.

VI: THE PACT

SS Sturmbannführer Lieffer, commandant of 84 Avenue Foch, had an interpreter, Ernst Vogt.[32] Swiss on his mother's side, and born and brought up where the Rhine was so narrow one could shout to friends and relations on the Swiss bank, Vogt was hardly a typical German and had, since he was twenty, lived in Paris, where he had worked as a clerk in a patent attorney's. Shortly after the outbreak of war, he was interned, at Pau, but when the Germans occupied France in 1940 he was released and required to report to a recruiting office in Paris. There he was recommended to go to 84 Avenue Foch, to be interpreter for Sturmbannführer Kieffer. In any case, his short-sightedness and colour-blindness would have excluded him from the army. He had never been a member of the Nazi party, and though he was now commissioned *Untersturmführer* (Second Lieutenant), never became a party member. Like Kieffer, he worked in civilian clothes. Of all the Germans, it was he whom I came to know by far the best. As a witness I found him honest — for which I had indeed been prepared by the French authorities — and testimonies as to his humanity are not lacking.

It was only after the arrest of Prosper and Archambaud that he was required to interpret between Kieffer and prisoners. In one of his letters to me he said:[33]

---

[32] Called Ernest in my earlier books. For a special study of Vogt, see my *Conversations with a Captor* (Fuller d'Arch Smith, 1973)

[33] Written October 27, 1958. We had had many conversations and much correspondence before this was written

Prosper and Archambaud refused to make any statement for forty-eight hours after their arrest, this to give time for the other members of their group to change domicile... During the forty-eight hours after their arrest, Prosper and Archambaud maintained a complete silence, refusing to make any statement, even to give their real names and nationalities. During those forty-eight hours, Scherer, von Kapri, Rühl, Goetz and I took it in relays to be with Prosper and Archambaud night and day separately (they were held separately in separate offices), and we had formal orders from Kieffer not to touch them, not to press them to make a statement and above all Kieffer ordered us not to subject them to any ill-treatment, to take our meals with them (the properly cooked meals that were brought to us), and to give them as many English cigarettes as they wanted (Archambaud did not smoke at all). None of us knew anything about Prosper and Archambaud, and we had for these forty-eight hours to keep on asking them the same question:

What is your real name and activity?

It was only at the end of these forty-eight hours that Kieffer intervened personally and showed them the photostatted copies of the reports they had sent to London and told them he knew all about their activity. IT WAS ONLY AFTER THIS THAT THE FAMOUS PACT WAS CONCLUDED BETWEEN Prosper and Kieffer.

Vogt put the matter briefly here, because he had told me verbally years before. Kieffer was able to cause dismay to Prosper and Archambaud by setting before them photocopies of the handwritten reports which they had sent to London, in clear, by the homebound aircraft, and also some aerial photographs of country houses which he said were the training schools in England. He was able to tell them the location of certain of the training schools, Arisaig, Scotland; Beaulieu, Hampshire (Vogt was puzzled by this name because it looked to him French, but Kieffer assured him [as the fact was] that there really was a place of this name in Hampshire, and told him how he must pronounce it to the English prisoners); Ringway, near Manchester (for parachute course) and the address of the headquarters of the French Section in London and the names of a number of the staff. This display of knowledge caused Prosper and Archambaud considerable despondency, but though they could see, obviously, that the mail had been betrayed by someone through whose hands it had passed before leaving France, they seemed to have it in their heads that there must have been a leak from London also. Neither Kieffer nor he suggested to them that there was a traitor in London, though when they saw the doubt was in their minds, obviously they did nothing to dissipate it, but rather played upon the possibility, as by saying meaningfully, 'Perhaps.' Indeed, Vogt did not know.

Kieffer told Prosper that in return for his telling him where the arms were piled and making it possible to collect them, he would guarantee that the members of his network would not be killed or ill-treated.

Prosper, plainly deeply troubled, turned to Vogt, and asked, 'Can I trust your chief?'

Vogt said, 'Yes.'

In retrospect, because of what happened after, he felt the responsibility for this weigh heavily upon him. 'Of course, I must have said, "Yes," in any case, to support my chief, but I feel if I had not said it with so much conviction he might have refused the bargain.' Vogt thought it was a good offer they were making him — to bring in the arms before they had been used to kill German soldiers, and by so doing win the lives of his own people. 'That gave me energy in explaining it.' He added words of his own, 'I know Mr Kieffer. You can trust Mr Kieffer.'

Prosper asked what authority Kieffer had to guarantee their lives. Kieffer accepted the question as reasonable and sent to Berlin for an authority. A paper arrived. Vogt saw it. 'This thing was stamped with the seal of the *Reichssicherheitshauptamt.*'

Prosper accepted it. Then Archambaud was brought in and shown it, too, and Prosper advised him to stand by the terms of it.

Vogt believed that Prosper acted in a serious spirit, gravely, and in the honest belief he was doing the best for his people, in the circumstances.

Nevertheless, there is a deposition from Joseph Placke, of Kieffer's staff, which makes distressing reading:

... Prosper declared himself arch-ready and to prove it gave the address of one of his colleagues, Darling, who lived at Gisors. He wrote Darling a letter asking him to yield the arms to bearer, so Langer[34] told me. Was it under constraint that Prosper gave this address? I do not know, for I was not present at that moment of the interrogation. When I was told about it by Langer, I was surprised at the facility with which he had 'sat down to the table'. I did not seek to know in what circumstance he has given away his comrade, Darling.

Major Kieffer ordered a lorry and two cars out to get the arms... Before we reached Darling's home,[35] the two cars drew away from the lorry. I was in one of them but believe what happened was that Darling accompanied the lorry on his motor-bicycle to a place in the Forest called Bois de l'Etoile.

---

[34] Another of Kieffer's staff

[35] I think he means Madame Guépin's home. Captain Darling, an officer left behind by the BEF and recruited into the *Prosper* network by Cuholi, made his home at or near Triechâteau and was unofficially engaged to Madame Guépin

The arms were there, and were loaded on to the lorry... Then Darling came out of the wood on his motorcycle. Prevost then fired... Darling saw that the lorry barred his way and made off through the woods. An hour later we found him lying wounded on the ground and Langer and I took him to the hospital at Gisors, where he was operated in my presence. Apart from some light wounds, he had a 6.3 or 6.5 bullet in the liver; I stayed by his bedside and he died the next day after shaking my hand. I telephoned Kieffer.

... When Prosper knew the result of what he had done, he realised too late that he had done a stupid thing, and in the interrogation which followed, at which I was not present, he gave away all the other arms dumps, together with the names of those holding them. In consequence of his talking, further expeditions were made during the following week, to collect arms and make arrests, notably at Méru, Creux, Evreux, and other places I cannot now remember.

I still remember the feeling of sickness which came over me when I first read this account, in the photocopy which tumbled out of an envelope sent me by the Abbé Guillaume of the certified copy (for Culioli's lawyer's file) of the deposition made by Joseph Placke on April 1, 1946, before Inspector Leon Jega of the DST at the request of the Juge d'Instruction Donsimoni. At the same time, experience has taught me to notice that whereas Vogt writes his testimonies in such a way as to leave his former prisoners as much of their dignity as possible, making the best of them, within the confines of truth, Placke makes the worst of them, charging them recklessly. In fairness, Prosper probably thought that by furnishing the Germans with a letter to Darling, instructing him to hand arms to bearer, he was avoiding the bloodshed that might result if Darling understood that he was in the face of the enemy and resisted. He may have thought that Darling, handing the arms over peacefully, to what he supposed members of the Resistance, would be left unmolested.

But how had Archambaud fared? He was the first prisoner whom Vogt interrogated other than in his function as Kieffer's interpreter, and it came about in this way. They had been questioning Archambaud during a morning, and when they broke off for lunch Kieffer said to Vogt, 'Why do we learn so little?'

'He did not expect an answer,' Vogt said to me, 'but I gave him one.' He told Kieffer that often he could see he was putting the questions at an angle oblique from what he wanted to know. 'But I cannot be in your head. I do not know what really you want to know. I do not know what you want to find out from these questions. So I repeat as the cure repeats the mass.'

Kieffer appreciated that it was unsatisfactory to do an interrogation through a third person, but he spoke no English and even his French was not good enough to allow him to do one without an interpreter. He asked Vogt if he thought he could do better by asking the questions on his own.

Vogt said he thought he could.

Kieffer said, 'But there is a method in it.' SS who were to become interrogators underwent a course of training. 'You have not been trained.' But then he reflected that if Vogt liked to try it could do no harm. 'There is nothing we can lose but our time, and that we lose already.' He would give Vogt the file on Archambaud. 'Is there anything else you want?'

'Tea.'

'Tea?'

Vogt said he wanted to be able to offer the prisoner some refreshment, to put him at his ease and loosen his tongue. Whisky would be no good, or any form of alcohol. As soon as the prisoner saw it he would know it was being offered him to make him talk; he would probably refuse it and in any case guard his words more closely than ever. 'But there will be no reaction against tea. The English like tea. Tea is harmless. It will relax him.' Before the war, Vogt had spent three weeks in England, au pair with a family in Tunbridge Wells, to practice speaking English. Sometimes he had been into the kitchen. 'I have seen tea made. I believe that I could make it myself, as the English make it.' He asked for milk, also, and sugar and a proper tea-set.

It could not have been easy to find tea, in wartime Paris. He did not know where they got it from. But somebody must have been sent on a mission to procure it, for a packet of tea appeared on his desk, with the other things he had asked for.

Over his lunch and during the early part of the afternoon, he studied the file. Then, about four o'clock, he unlocked the door of Archambaud's cell, and asked, 'Will you have tea with me?'

He tried to make it like a pleasant interlude between interrogations, rather than an interrogation, and wrote nothing down while Archambaud was with him, storing in his memory whatever seemed interesting. But afterwards he had something to write down and to show to Kieffer. Kieffer was pleased with it and said, 'If you can always do as well as this, you can do all the interrogations.'[36]

He interrogated all the major agents of the French Section, that is to say, the organisers, and the radio-operators on the nontechnical side of their work. The technical side was done by Dr Goetz, the radio expert of the Avenue Foch. The

---

[36] Vogt to myself verbally, during one of our first meetings, in June 1950 See my *Conversations with a Captor* (Fuller d'Arch Smith, 1973) pp 24-25

couriers Vogt hardly saw, their interrogation being done by August Scherer, a civil auxiliary like himself, a schoolmaster by profession, and the one with whom Vogt felt most in common.

From Dr Goetz, he heard that Archambaud had given his code and security-check, using which a radio message had been sent to London, and that the reply message which came from London was *You forgot your double security-check be more careful.* He placed this before Archambaud, who was quite overthrown by shock and dismay.

Archambaud had good reason to be upset. Goetz knew there had to be a security check; what he did not know was that in Archambaud's case there had to be two. Archambaud had been told the first security check, like the code, might be ceded, absence of the second indicating he was in German hands.

What was the mentality of the people in London who made the blundering reply that gave the game away? That the story is true, I have no doubt. It was not only Vogt who told it to me. I was told it by two men, John Starr and Yeo-Thomas, who were later to become fellow prisoners of Archambaud and were told it by him. Also, Goetz, when a prisoner after the year, put it in his statement for the British authorities, according to Professor Foot (official history, p. 329).

What is also certain is that this piece of stupidity did more than anything else to undermine Archambaud's morale. He simply could not get over it, and talked about it to everybody, not only to fellow prisoners with whom he was able to snatch the chance of a word, but even to Vogt. It put him into a mood of blaming London and confiding in his interrogator.

Vogt told me of another incident:[37]

---

[37] Vogt to author, in letter dated October 10, 1954.

One day 'Archambaud' was all on edge, and to my question, 'What is the matter?' he replied. 'Mr Goetz has given me, in clear, the text of a radiophonic message I received from London several weeks before my arrest. He had received the deciphered text of the message from Berlin. Now that was a message I had never been able to decipher myself, as London had committed a fault in the ciphering. Well, in Berlin they had deciphered it, and so it is from the Germans that I learn what it contained.' I know that the central department in Berlin recorded almost all the enemy radiophonic messages from France and elsewhere, and that every time we arrested a radio operator Kieffer immediately asked Berlin to send, still ciphered or deciphered, the texts of the messages which he had sent to and received from London. For a long time after that 'Archambaud' racked his brains as to how Berlin had been able to decipher his messages.

This passage seems to support the Abbé Guillaume's belief that the arrival of the two Canadians by parachute in the Sologne was known to the Germans through their having broken Archambaud's code, while he was still at liberty.[38] Germaine Tambour, two days before her arrest, had told Laure Lebras the Germans seemed to know of parachutings at the same time as the Resistance and she believed they had the code.[39] Professor Foot wrote that he had seen no evidence causing him to believe the Germans ever broke the code of an operator still at liberty,[40] but Professor Foot had not the benefit of having seen Vogt's letter to me about this. That they asked the agents to give their codes may seem evidence against their ability to break them, but I suspect it may have been a question of time. From Vogt's letter, it appears to me that

----

[38] Abbé Guillaume to author, verbally, May 16, 1955
[39] Madame Lebras to author, verbally, November 25, 1955.
[40] Official history, p. 105.

sometimes they could and sometimes they could not break the code.

Vogt said to me many times that he did not regard Prosper and Archambaud as traitors. Both, he felt, were naturally straight men, caught in a situation in which the ground seemed to have gone from under them. Speaking of Archambaud, he stressed his superior intelligence and gentleness of character. Nevertheless, there was obviously something connected with Archambaud which troubled him.

'For the Resistants, Archambaud appeared as the great traitor,' he said. That was partly because they did not see Prosper, but only Archambaud, who told them about the pact, and perhaps they thought he had invented it. Prosper had been taken away from the Avenue Foch as soon as it had been concluded. Kieffer told Vogt it was because Berlin had asked for Prosper, and Vogt supposed it was because they wanted to continue questioning of Prosper at higher level. The result was that it was Archambaud who was left to face new prisoners as they were brought in and explain to them that Prosper and he had concluded an agreement with the Germans to hand everything over and to advise them in their turn to cooperate in the spirit of the pact.

Vogt was emphatic that Archambaud did not desire a German victory. On the contrary, Archambaud was always saying, 'When I return to London after the war I shall demand an Inquiry into the conduct of the French Section.' But in the meantime, he did most things that were asked of him.

'It was unfortunate he had such a good memory,' Vogt said. Most people forgot a good many things, genuinely. 'If he had said sometimes, "I can't remember", I might have believed him.'

'Also,' he said, 'there were some episodes.'

At least one of these was very innocent in intention and perhaps in result. Vogt told me the story during our first meetings, in June 1950, but I take the account from one of his later letters:[41]

> I regret that Archambaud is dead. As I have already said he was a man of a superior intelligence and an honest man. He gave me his word of honour not to attempt to escape so long as he was with me. I had his word and thought no more about it. During the time he was with me he never attempted to escape, although there were several very favourable occasions. Once I went out alone with him at night (between 9 and 10) to a small villa in a suburb of Paris to look for one of his wireless sets, and I did not know what I should meet in that villa. I had such confidence in his word that I risked everything. He did not want to give us the address of the villa or the name of the people living in it. But he wanted to go with me to it to look for the set. He told me the villa belonged to an elderly couple, that the woman was very ill (heart trouble) and that it would be enough to kill her if German police suddenly arrived and raided the place to look for the set. He said that these people did riot know that it was a radio-set, which by the way was not true. It was only on my promise that we should make no reprisals against the aged couple that Archambaud consented to go with me to look for the set. He said it was better for us to disembarrass these people of the radio-set before German police found it in their house. Moreover he knew we had several sets of this type already and that it was without importance whether we had one more or less. At that time, he still did not believe that we would succeed in making transmissions to London.

41 Vogt, letter to author, September 12, 1954

Archambaud, Vogt said, transmitted extremely fast, which was why he did not believe that any of the Germans' operators could successfully imitate his sending. In fact, Vogt said, it was two brothers, French, *les frères Ledanseurs*, who worked Archambaud's set back to London. But if I understand rightly, the set Archambaud went out with Vogt to collect was not the operational one — with the crystals in it — so that truly it was rather to oblige Kieffer's desire for tidiness that it was brought in, rather than for a more sinister purpose. Vogt had a sentiment for the story, because he felt that he had risked his life in going out with a British prisoner alone — who might not simply have run away from him but led him into an ambush in which he would be killed — but I relate it because the light it sheds on Archambaud's way of thinking and feeling helps one to understand more sympathetically his role in a story which Vogt did not tell me, but which I am sure had in mind when he said that there were "episodes", and which has been cited against Archambaud in three works:

The story is this: Archambaud arrived in an open car with three German civilians at the home of Madame Arend, the sister of Denise, and asked for a radio-set he had left there. Her husband was out, but his father handed over the set, and, taking it for granted the Germans had been bribed or won over by Archambaud, and never dreaming he was a prisoner in their hands, volunteered to fetch his son, who would know where to find parts of it that were missing. He had the imprudence to mention his son was a *refractaire*. By the time the son, Robert Arend, arrived, the Germans as well as Archambaud were being offered drinks and cigarettes. The Germans then asked to see Robert Arend's papers, and when they left in the car Archambaud went with them. A few days afterwards, Robert Arend was arrested. This unhappy story, told by Madame

Arend to Elizabeth Nicholas, I first read in her book[42] but it appears again in the official history, in the words of Robert Arend, found by Professor Foot on his personal file — for he returned from Buchenwald.[43]

Although it makes such painful reading, I feel that the spirit in which Archambaud would have gone out is illuminated by what Vogt told me of his own expedition *à deux* with Archambaud. With reference to that, he told me verbally that he told Archambaud he should not give the aged couple any indication that he was under arrest or that his relationship with himself [Vogt] was that of prisoner to captor. He said to him, 'Don't say I'm from the Gestapo!' he told him he could say he was a friend, or just 'This is Ernest', or even nothing at all, to explain the extra presence. It would save the couple a heart attack.

The same reasoning must have governed Archambaud's going with the Germans to the Arends' and not explaining the situation. In speaking to Archambaud, Vogt told me he always presented whatever he wanted him to do as being for the avoidance of violence; but of course, while this was true, there was always another side to it, which was that if the people visited did not understand they were being visited by the enemy, there was the chance they might give away something of interest. (The pattern was one which repeated, not only in the case of Archambaud.)

One must say, however, that it was foolish of Mr Arend, senior, to compromise his son before Germans, of whom he knew nothing, even if he did take it for granted Archambaud had somehow or other got them on his side.

---

⁴² *Death Be Not Proud*, (Cresset, 1958), pp 178-79
⁴³ Official history, p 318

When I went to see the Abbé Guillaume, he told me Archambaud had virtually 'participated' in the arrest of Dr. Helmer, as of Robert Arend, and counted amongst others given away by Archambaud the Comte and Comtesse de Bernard, M. et Mme. Flamencourt and Jean and Guy Dutems. The Comte de Bernard was startled when during his interrogation at Avenue Foch he was told they had had tripe for dinner on the last occasion Archambaud dined with them (which was true). Madame Flamencourt had testified (Culioli file, f. 109) that while a prisoner she had spoken to Germaine Tambour who had told her she was shaken to see Archambaud looking very much at ease at Avenue Foch, pouring out tea, and showing the Germans on a map the fields where parachute deliveries were made, and that he practically took part in her interrogation, saying, 'But Germaine, you haven't told them this... you haven't told them that...', defeating her efforts to keep some things back. (The Tambour sisters had been arrested two months before Prosper and

Archambaud, so they must have been kept under interrogation for a long time.) A Monsieur Gounu testified (25.2.51), 'I have hardly known a more painful moment in my life than when, on July 4, 1943, Gilbert Norman (Archambaud) came towards me at 84 Avenue Foch and said with the most complete poise (*désinvolture*), "You can tell them everything... they are stronger than we are."'

The Abbé showed me his own copies of these and other adverse testimonies when I went to see him and afterwards sent me copies of his copies.

Madame Balachowsky told me that when the SS came to Grignon, eighty strong, on July 1, their leader told Monsieur Vandervynct, the Director, it was 'Gilbert' Archambaud who had given them all away, and produced a list of the names —

Balachowsky at the head — of the men who had been to meet a parachute delivery at Roncey-aux-Alluets. The list of the men composing the team was exactly correct, as was the number of the parachutes they had brought back on a lorry to Grignon, to bury: seven. They also stated that 'a young English girl, recently arrived, calling herself Jeanne-Marie' had been at Grignon. This was a reference to Madeleine, whose cover-name was Jeanne-Marie Regnier. Now, Madeleine had been received on her arrival by Déricourt and I incline to think he would have notified the Germans. Nevertheless, it would have been her operational name, Madeleine, which would have been given him by London. It is unlikely he would have known her cover-name was Jeanne-Marie and impossible he could know she had been to Grignon, as he was not a member of the *Prosper* network and knew nothing of Grignon. Only two people could have known and told the Germans that 'Jeanne-Marie' had been at Grignon, Archambaud and Denise. Denise is not known to have talked. I find it impossible not to believe, with Madame Balachowsky, that it was Archambaud, who had conducted Madeleine from Paris to Grignon, who had told the Germans.

Madame Balachowsky had been informed by a certain 'Jean' of Prosper's arrest, by telephone, within two hours of its having taken place, and of the arrest of Archambaud and Denise and she had at once telephoned Madeleine, who had radioed the news of the disaster to London that same day; it was therefore incomprehensible to Madame Balachowsky that London should have discounted Madeleine's intelligence of the arrest of Archambaud and replied to the message sent by the Germans over his radio, *You forgot your double-security check be more careful.*

Déricourt told me that on June 25 he saw Archambaud and Denise being led out of the latter's lodgings in the rue des Petites Ecuries in handcuffs — they might have been taken there to fetch some things — and sent a message to London through the radio-operator Dowlen saying Prosper, Archambaud and Denise arrested. That intelligence of the disaster was received from Déricourt via Dowlen is confirmed in Professor Foot, official history, p. 322.

Madeleine, very scared, had come to see the Balachowskys at their home at Viroflay the day before the SS went to Grignon, and they had warned her not even to return to the Garrys without first telephoning to make sure their flat was not already occupied by the Gestapo. She went immediately to their telephone, and Madame Balachowsky had to say, 'Not from here, so that the number can be traced! Do it from a public callbox; and if you are answered by a man whose voice you don't know, who says he is a friend of Garry, take it the flat is occupied already by the Gestapo and don't go.'

In fact, it was occupied by the Gestapo already. The Garrys were out when they came, and on their return their concierge was able to intercept them and tell them a lot of men had gone up to their flat, so they took it that this was the Gestapo and simply slipped away. Vogt told me that they did in fact go to the Garrys' flat that day (I think he said he was one of the party) and that had either Madeleine or the Garrys entered they would certainly have been arrested.

At Grignon, the SS arrested the Director, Vandervynct, his son-in-law, Douillet, who had been one of the parachute reception team, and some others, and a detachment of about 15 men went to the farm at Roncey-les-Alluets, where they terrified the farmer's wife, Madame Abgral, by putting her and her children against a wall, saying they would shoot them all unless they told them where her husband was, and raising their automatics as though they were going to do it. In fact, they were not so wicked as actually to shoot, but Monsieur Abgral, though not given away, was arrested when he came home of his own accord. After that, they encamped on the place, and in the course of the summer obliged Madame Abgral to provide them with meals when they came there to organise, on two occasions, parachute receptions; obviously, they were using Archambaud's code and radio-set to arrange with London for deliveries. As Madame Abgral was not allowed to go outside during these operations, she did not know whether human beings came down into German hands, or only containers. One of the Germans told her, 'It is Gilbert who gave you away,' and added, 'His real name is Norman.' This was information, to her, as to her as to all sub-agents of the Prosper network, Archambaud was known only as 'Gilbert'.

Nevertheless, Madame Balachowsky, though not pleased with Archambaud (her own husband was arrested on July 2 and spent the rest of the war in Buchenwald), thought she ought in fairness to mention to me that prior to Archambaud's arrest, while he was at Grignon, in fact, on the day of the Fete of Grignon, when he was to transmit at 5.00 pm, the Minister of Agriculture arrived together with the chief of Police, and the latter took Vandervynct aside and told him that 'certain departments know that something is going on here,' and advised him to make it disappear before arrests took place.

When Madame Balachowsky plucked up the courage to go to the Avenue Foch, after her husband's arrest, to find if there was anything she could do to help him, she was received by Vogt, whom she described to me as, 'a charming boy', and he said to her, 'Your husband has somebody near to him whom he thinks of as a friend but who is not one.' She racked her brains to think who this could be, but it was not until after the war she learned of the virulent professional jealousy of a scientific man, whom her husband had to some extent taken into his confidence concerning his Resistance work, and putting two and two together she came to believe it was he to whom Vogt had been referring; therefore she supposed that at least some leaks came from that quarter.[44]

It must also be mentioned that Cohen ('Justin') who had been parachuted on to the field at Roncey-aux-Alluets just before the disaster, had an appointment with Archambaud on the morning of June 24 — a few hours after he had been arrested. He did not come. Had he turned instant traitor, he could have brought the Gestapo to his rendezvous with Cohen, so Cohen's witness is confirmation for Vogt's statement that during the first 48 hours Archambaud gave nothing away. Cohen, disturbed by the failure of Archambaud to keep the appointment, told Weil, who made investigations and then told him to radio London saying Archambaud had been arrested. This Cohen did, and received a reply from London YOU MUST BE MISTAKEN BECAUSE ARCHAMBAUD IS STILL TRANSMITTING TO US. When Cohen gave that to Weil, Weil made him reply, IF ARCHAMBAUD IS STILL TRANSMITTING HE IS A TRAITOR AS HE IS UNDER ARREST.

One is stupefied again by the apparent absolute inability of London to grasp the fact that Archambaud had, as Madeleine had told them, as Déricourt had told them, as Cohen had told

---

[44] I take all these details from a series of extremely long letters written to me by Madame Balachowsky between December 1 and December 20, 1958 Nevertheless, I had had a number of meetings with her, and also with her husband, and correspondence with both of them, from 1949 onwards

them, been arrested and it was the Germans who were working the set.

How many people were altogether arrested in the *Prosper* disaster? It is most often said, 500. Madame Balachowsky told me she considered this far too low. By her own count, which took into consideration a continuing wave, starting from June 24 and sweeping on through July and August, with extensions from Paris and the Loire valley into Brittany, the arrests ran to 1,500. Professor Foot writes, '400 would be a conservative estimate'.[45] Déricourt always referred to the number at 540. Whatever the exact figure — and even if the most conservative estimate be entertained — it was, to the best of my knowledge and belief numerically the worst disaster suffered by the clandestine services in the war.

These were not, of course, all given away by one person. I do not think that even the most bitter of Archambaud's critics conceived that he stored in his head and gave the Germans that number of names and addresses. Madame Balachowsky wrote to me:[46]

> There were close to Prosper illumined spirits like Denise, arrested with her briefcase in which she was carrying names and addresses, which made possible the arrest of so many persons, amongst others that of Edouard Herriot, with whom we had been put in relation by Jerome Tharaud, so that he could go to London; she had that name and address in her briefcase when she was arrested.

Though it was unlucky she had this list of names and addresses in her briefcase when she was arrested, Denise appears not to have talked, or at any rate not to have talked

---

[45] Official history, p 321
[46] Madame Balachowsky to author, June 12, 1957

more than she could help, under interrogation. I asked Vogt about her; he said guardedly, 'She did as well as she knew how; in that sense, one can say she did well.' She seems to have been scandalised by the pact. After a day or two at the Avenue Foch she was removed to Fresnes, and from there, through the kindness of a wardress, probably Trude Scherer, she was able to send letters to her sister, Madame Arend. In these letters, she wrote very bitterly that Gilbert had given them all away; though she also added that he was affording her some protection.[47] Madame Arend only knew one Gilbert, and that was Archambaud, whom Denise had sometimes brought to the house.

Worms and Guerne and the latter's wife were arrested on July 1 at the restaurant 'Chez Tutulle', to which it was folly for them to have returned after the disaster. It was here that, with the visit of Christmann, the downfall of the *Prosper* network had begun. The proprietors, M. and Mme. Touret, were arrested with them. Weil, arriving late for lunch, saw them being led away.

Déricourt told me Worms refused absolutely to talk at all, 'although he was very badly beaten up, less for his refusal to divulge information than for his arrogant manner towards the Germans.' I never asked Déricourt his source for this information. It could only be German, and I supposed Boemelburg had told him.

---

[47] Letter from Madame Arend to Elizabeth Nicholas, 1959 Madame Arend had lent the letters to a Major Mackenzie, by whom she was visited after the war, so that they might be copied in London, and wished that she had received them back Dame Irene Ward took this up with the Foreign Office, who traced and questioned Major Mackenzie, but he was unable to remember having received the letters

Guerne asked and obtained the permission to speak with Archambaud, whom he had known before the war, at Avenue Foch. He told me Archambaud told him that Prosper and he had made the pact purely in order to benefit the members of the network; that his and Prosper's own lives were not purchased by it, only the lives of the others. This does not tally with Vogt's testimony.

Another who was arrested on July 1 was Maurice Lequeux, chief of a sub-network on the north bank of the Loire, roughly facing Culioli's operational area on the south bank. After the war Lequeux was to be charged with having led the Gestapo, after his arrest, round the villages near the Chaigny power station, indicating the arms dumps and pointing out persons who had given any help, so that they could be arrested; giving it is said, needless particulars concerning a particular piece of past sabotage, and even, whilst at Fresnes prison, three weeks after the interrogations were over, he asked to be heard again in order to furnish the Gestapo with some bits of information he had previously forgotten.

We left Culioli at the Avenue Foch, where he had been brought briefly, from Blois, on the night of the arrest of Archambaud and Denise. Later the same night he was taken to Fresnes, and from there to the Hôpital de la Pitié. There he was visited on July 1 or 2 by an inspector of police in the German service, who told him they had an agent in the top office in London, and knew the whole organisation. They followed the steps of Déricourt, he said, and added for good measure, 'I myself took part in the reception of Madeleine, and of another operation by Hudson...' They knew the letterbox in which he received letters from London; they knew the messages which would announce the Invasion.

Culioli was wise enough not to take any of this as necessarily true. Nevertheless, the inspector laid out before him a Michelin map, on which were marked sixteen of his parachute receiving fields, the latest sixteen accepted by London. He then showed him photocopies of a great mass of papers, both handwritten and typed, reports of sabotage, instructions from London, both in English and in German translation. Culioli was not permitted to do more than glance through them, but the amplitude of the collection convinced him it must have preceded the arrest of Prosper, Archambaud and Denise, and must have been drawn from the direction of the network.

With regard to photocopied mail, we shall talk about it later; but note that, while Déricourt was almost certainly responsible for that, he could not have been for the marked map. Déricourt had nothing to do with parachute operations and would have had no idea where Culioli's fields were. In order to arrange with London for their use, however, radio messages had to be sent to London giving the geographical coordinates and other particulars, and these messages, like the replies from London, went over Archambaud's radio-set. We already have the hearsay evidence of Germaine Tambour, reported by Madame Flamencourt, that Archambaud showed the Germans the parachute fields on a map, but sixteen does seem to me rather a lot to have remembered exactly and I do not altogether dismiss the possibility the Germans were able to understand his radio messages while he was still at liberty.

The inspector then told Culioli of the pact concluded by Prosper and invited him to subscribe to it. Culioli asked to be allowed to see Prosper, but was told it was not possible. Instead, Archambaud was brought in to him, in handcuffs but looking perfectly at ease.

'It is true,' said Archambaud. He explained that the Germans had obviously known all about their activities for a long while, but that they had promised no one should be shot providing all the arms received from London were handed over.

The German inspector said that every weapon must be brought in, down to the last pistol.

'Impossible,' said Archambaud, 'the greater number have been distributed.'

Culioli said, 'None of mine have been distributed. There have been too many dangerous incidents. The lot are piled in a few places.' This was untrue, but he hoped by giving a display of cooperation and sacrificing a small number to save the rest.

On the following morning Culioli gave the addresses of Couffrant of Romorantin, responsible for 30 containers, Gatignon of Moyer-sur-Cher, responsible for 20 containers, Cordelet of Chaumont-sur-Loire, responsible for 25 containers and Le Meur of Chambord, responsible for 14 containers. The 90 thus sacrificed were less than half of the total.

He wrote a letter to each of the four men saying he was sorry to have to give them away, explaining the pact and asking them to hand over their arms without compromising more people than necessary. He added a sentence recommending that if the arms dumps were mined, care should be taken the Wehrmacht were not injured. The dumps were not mined, but he thought this expression of thought for the safety of their men should put the Germans in the best mood. And he signed the four letters.

It is this signing of the letters, making clear the situation, to the four persons given away, that in my eyes raises Culioli above those who let their comrades be compromised unawares. It shows straightforwardness and responsibility.

A few days later, Langer brought him a letter from Archambaud saying that he must have six radio-sets, of which only five had been found. Where was the sixth?

Culioli pretended to think that Archambaud himself had taken it. In fact, the Comte de Bernard had put it in a sack and stuffed into an underwater hole in the bank of the Cosse, from which he retrieved it after his return from concentration camp at the end of the war.

But now the four householders were each, in their turn, faced with the problem of how far he should fall in with the pact. Under threat of reprisals against the people of his village Couffrant wrote a letter for the Germans to take to the man storing a sub-depot of the arms, and this person in his turn was arrested together with his wife.

VII: SUMMER 1943

We left Déricourt at the Gare d'Austerlitz, where, on June 21, Prosper handed over to him for repatriation the shot-down English airman, Taylor. On the 23, he and Marc took their charges, Heslop and the airman, to Amboise. Normally Déricourt arranged that he and Marc should travel by an earlier train than their passengers, and meet them with bicycles. On this occasion, however, they all went on the same train, Déricourt and the airman in one carriage, Marc and Heslop in another. As the airman spoke not a word of French, he was told to pretend to be asleep during the four hour train journey, so as not to have to chat either to his companion or to other passengers. Actually, the whole operation was under German protection, but Déricourt could not tell Marc this, or his passengers, so they had to go through the charade of elaborate security.

Déricourt and Taylor went first through the barrier, where a gendarme studied the airman's papers for a painfully long time, before waving him on. Déricourt and Marc got out the four bicycles they had earlier deposited at the consigne, then they all cycled to the tiny village of Pocé-sur-Cisse, slightly east of the town, on the north bank of the Loire. Thirty years later, Rémy Clément (Marc) showed me the inn where they had had dinner at a table in the garden. As the airman could not pretend to be asleep all through dinner, and it would look unnatural if the other three left him wholly out of their conversation, and he could not produce even a word in answer if the waiter asked him anything, they now pretended he was deaf. 'It's no good saying anything to him,' they told the people at the next table.

'He was deafened by the British bombing of Nantes.' This caused great interest and solicitude. After it was dark, they cycled to the edge of the field. Marc showed me the clump of bushes near the road behind which they hid their bicycles. Déricourt and Marc set out the lights. In the small hours of the morning of June 24, the Lysander from London, piloted by Hugh Verity, came down. Two men stepped out. Heslop and Taylor stepped aboard, with parting expressions of gratitude to Déricourt and Marc.

Déricourt and Marc handed bicycles to the two men who had descended from the Lysander, told them that a train left Amboise station for Paris at 8.30 am and advised them to make themselves comfortable until then, and parted from them.

Déricourt and Marc went back to rest at the small Hotel St. Victoire, which Marc showed me, at Pocé-sur-Cisse, where they took a room on nights when they used the Pocé field. Shortly before 8.30, they strolled on to the station platform at Amboise. They saw and were seen by the two men who had come from London, but no recognition signs were exchanged. The train came in, and was boarded by all four, Déricourt and Marc sitting in one compartment, Robert Lyon and Colonel Bonoteaux in another. From time to time, Déricourt and Marc passed the compartment in which the other two were sitting, in the corridor.

Arriving in Paris at the Gare d'Austerlitz at about mid-day, Déricourt and Marc walked off on their own, and Lyon and Bonoteaux went their separate directions, each followed by members of the Bony-Lafont gang, shadowing them on behalf of the Gestapo, which had taken notes of their appearance on the platform at Amboise and ridden up in the train with them, in different compartments.

Lyon went to an address near the Porte de la Vilette. The men of the Bony-Lafont team, having seen him enter the building, were ordered to discontinue trailing him. He afterwards went to the Gare de Lyons, from which he took the train to Lyons, where he assumed the command of a network.

Colonel Bonoteaux took the metro from the Gare d'Austerlitz to the Porte d'Auteuil, where he got out and walked, followed by the men from the Bony-Lafont team, to a block of flats where he rang a bell. The bell was that of his sister (or sister-in-law). Receiving no reply, he walked back to the Porte d'Auteuil metro station, reentered the metro, still followed by the men of the Bony-Lafont gang, and returned to the Gare d'Austerlitz. There, the gang, thinking he was going to take the main line train again, arrested him, and took him to their headquarters on the rue Lauriston.

Colonel Bonoteaux was not a member of SOE but of the ORA, and in his briefcase were found papers showing his relations with General Olleris, captured almost a fortnight earlier. General Olleris had been bluffing, minimising his anti-German activities; when these papers were found on Colonel Bonoteaux, his bluff fell.[48]

---

[48] It was Robert Lyon who, when he came to see me on March 27, 1959, after the publication of my *Double Webs*, told me the story not only of his own movements after arrival at the Gare St Lazare but those of Bonoteaux, as the latter had told them to a fellow prisoner who had survived, and who was Lyon's source These reported testimonies, told by one prisoner to another, 'in case you survive and I do not', and carefully memorised, are very much a feature of Resistance history Bonoteaux felt that he had been trailed, and wanted the historians of the future to be able to work out how his doom had come on him. That his sense of being followed was not illusory can be seen from the detailed account of the shadowing, from the point of view of the Bony-Lafont gang, given in the statement of Pierre Bony to the DST on September 10, 1945.

That the trailing by the Bony-Lafont gang was the consequence of information laid by Déricourt is not a matter for doubt. In his deposition of November 1946 for the DST Déricourt declared having given away an operation which he thought was at Pocé-sur-Cisse, though he said he did not know if anyone had been arrested and indeed may not have known. He had not specifically wanted Bonoteaux to be arrested — Bony's deposition makes plain his team acted on its own initiative when the man they were under orders merely to trail acted in an unexpected manner, causing them to fear losing him — but, of course, in as much as Déricourt had made the trailing possible, this arrest was one for which he had in after years to recognise moral responsibility.

The morning of the Pocé-sur-Cisse operation was the morning on which Prosper was arrested. At the hour when the Avenue Foch men arrived at the Hotel Mazagran, Déricourt would have been standing about on or near the field at Pocé-sur-Cisse, with Marc, Heslop and Taylor, waiting for the aircraft; and at the moment when Prosper re-entered the Hotel Mazagran and was arrested, Déricourt would have been on the train, between Amboise and Paris, with Marc, Lyon and Bonoteaux.

Déricourt could not have given away the Hotel Mazagran address of Prosper, a new one, which Prosper had not told to even such close colleagues as Professor and Madame Balachowsky, Madame Guépin, Culioli or Guerne; Archambaud and Denise were the only persons to whom it would have been proper for him to give it.

Vogt made me a handwritten statement[49] that Kieffer gave him photostats of the mail sent by Prosper, Archambaud and

---

[49] Vogt, statement made for author, November 13, 1954, reproduced in *Double Webs* (Putnam, 1958), pp 41-43, and in *The Chequered Spy* (to

their colleagues to London, which were marked in the corner BOE 48, the reference number meaning 48th agent of Boemelburg; that Kieffer told him BOE 48 was Gilbert, the man charged by London with receiving and dispatching aircraft from London which landed in France, receiving agents who landed and boarding those due to depart, together with the mail from agents in the field; it was, Vogt said, this betrayal of the mail, which contained much information about their activities, addresses and so on, which enabled the Germans to bring off their big *coup de filet*, their round up of the Prosper network.

However, when I showed this statement, informally, over a dinner-table, to Colonel Mercier of the Tribunal Militaire Permanent de Paris, he observed to me that while it appeared to him to have been made honestly, it included a certain amount of hearsay — for what Kieffer told Vogt was in the legal sense hearsay — Vogt had not the capacity to stand cross-examination on the truth of what Kieffer told him — and the final paragraph constituted a passage from evidence to supposition. Vogt could not know that Kieffer did not know of the activities and addresses of Prosper, Archambaud and their colleagues from sources other than the betrayed mail.

Mercier's words were to be proved prophetic. After the publication of my *Double Webs*, Vogt wrote to me saying, 'I am no longer so sure of the guilt of Gilbert.' The intervention of Christmann and Bodens, and their meetings with Archambaud, Denise, Agazarian and other members of the Prosper group had been unknown to him. He had now to suppose that the arrest of Prosper, Archambaud and their colleagues was above all the consequence of that intervention. He began to think

---

appear as a George Mann Original, 1975)

now that Gilbert (Déricourt) 'rendered greater service to London than he did harm'.[50]

Meanwhile, Bleicher was working his way further into the large *Frager* network. He arranged the arrest of Frager's second in command, Sager, in the hope that Frager would promote Roger Bardet to be his second in command. This he did. As Bardet reported everything to Bleicher, Bleicher now had a pretty complete picture of all that was going on.

He now introduced Kiki (Raoul Kiffer) to Bardet. Kiki, since he first went over to the Germans after being given away by the Cat, had been used in Normandy. In the Lisieux area, he built up a fictitious Resistance network, in to which he drew all genuine Resistants. In other words, Kiki was a supreme agent provocateur, drawing out local talent for Resistance work and placing it under German control, so that it could be mopped up if it threatened to become dangerous. In the early summer of 1943, Bleicher introduced Kiki to Bardet who introduced him to Frager, and Kiki's German controlled network, known as the *Lisiana*, was affiliated to the *Frager* network.

A genuine British agent, Hercule, acted as radio operator to Frager, and regular parachute deliveries of arms, munitions and other cargoes were made from London. These were received, most often, by genuine Resistants, except in one district, where Bleicher, Bardet and Kiki formed part of the reception committee. In the other districts, Bardet or Kiki went afterwards to make an inventory of the cargoes and note the place of storage, so that under some pretext cargoes could later be removed and given into German custody.

A time came when Bleicher decided he must meet Frager, and a rendezvous was arranged in the Café Monte Carlo.

---

[50] Vogt, letter to author, October 27, 1958, reproduced in *Double Agent?* (Pan Books, 1961), pp. 186-88.

Bardet presented Bleicher to Frager as 'Colonel Henri', a German sympathetic to the Allies, and Frager, unaware that Bleicher knew everything about him from Bardet, represented himself as being Bardet's uncle.

Bleicher offered Frager information of interest to the Allies, and when he felt he had his confidence, as an earnest of the importance of the information he could give, told him Gilbert (Déricourt) was an agent of the Gestapo.

I have always supposed Bleicher's motive in doing this was to get Déricourt out of the way, so that Bardet could be supreme. Obviously, it was not in the German national interest for a German to give away a German agent to the Allies; but there was the rivalry between the Abwehr and the SD, though I doubt if Bleicher was so much concerned with that as with the extension of his own power through the elimination of the agent of the rival service.

Déricourt, himself, was much intrigued as to why Bleicher had given him away. Begging the question whether he was a real German agent, the point he made to me was that for Bleicher to give away a real SD agent, even allowing for the rivalry between the services, would have been a prodigious risk, unless he had behind him the authority of his own chiefs to make this leak — and if they authorised it, why? At any rate, Déricourt thought this question ought to have troubled Frager; he ought to have asked himself what the Germans hoped to get out of him, since they were sacrificing so much to him. 'If one is to be a double one should not be naive.' Nothing was given for nothing in spying. 'He should have asked himself what was the *contre-partie.*'

Myself, I think it was Bleicher's megalomania at work. He meant, certainly, by disclosing to Frager Déricourt's relations with the Germans, to increase Frager's trust in him, the more thoroughly to exploit it to the German advantage, but he wanted, also, by discrediting Déricourt with London, to have the exploitation of the Allied networks all to himself.

Whilst Agazarian was in London, Madeleine transmitted for Déricourt, and it was she who sent and received all the radio messages between him and London concerning the next operation, the reception of a Lysander on a vast, fen-flat field Marc had found in the Angers district, close by the village of Soucelles. The operation was on July 20. From it stepped Isadore Newman ('Pepe') and another, and on it Déricourt boarded Major Antelme ('Antoine') and a French lawyer named Savy. Then he boarded it himself, and paid an unofficial visit to London, which he spent in André Simon's flat, not, so he told me, disclosing his presence to Baker Street. He returned by parachute the following night.

Three days later, in the very early hours of July 23, at Soucelles again, Déricourt and Marc received a Hudson. From it stepped Major Nicholas Bodington, Buckmaster's second in command, and Agazarian, who had returned as Bodington's radio operator. On it were boarded three members of SOE Belgian Section.

Déricourt installed Bodington in Claire's flat off the Place des Ternes; it was really the flat of Jean Besnard, with whom she was now living and after an eventual divorce from Aisner after the war married. Besnard, a lawyer, was in the Resistance in the passive sense that he would allow his property to be used, to hide a radio set or an agent. Agazarian was installed by Déricourt in the flat of another friend, nearby. Déricourt's own flat was awkward as Bleicher had taken a flat for Suzanne Laurant in the house next door.

Bodington had come to France 'to see what was left', because there had been 'conflicting reports'.[51]

Professor Foot found on the files exposed to him while writing the official history (p. 330) that Antelme, on his return to London, declared that Archambaud was 'still free as messages continued to come from him' and assured Miss Penelope Tor (Information Officer to Buckmaster) that Archambaud 'would have shot himself rather than talk or transmit under duress,' against which Buckmaster wrote, 'Agree'. This is very perplexing, because Antelme was with Madeleine at the Garrys' flat at the time of the mass arrests and both fled it to take refuge in Madame Aigrain's flat, so that whatever Madeleine knew, he knew. One must, of course, beware of looking with hindsight. There were no newspapers to list the names of the persons arrested. But Madeleine had been sent out to assist Archambaud and would certainly know he had disappeared. Moreover, Madame Balachowsky, who had been informed of Prosper's arrest by a telephone call from a double-agent, Jean, within an hour of its having happened, told Madeleine that same day. Madame Balachowsky is positive that on that same day, also, June 25, Madeleine transmitted to London intelligence that Prosper, Archambaud and Denise had been arrested. How then can Antelme, in hiding with Madeleine in Madame Aigrain's flat, not have known? Perhaps what happened is that at Baker Street he was assured Archambaud was still transmitting to them and, momentarily nonplussed, could only imagine that Archambaud had, unknown to Madeleine and himself, escaped the holocaust.

It had indeed been noticed, found Professor Foot, that there had been a gap in Archambaud's transmissions, and that when

---

[51] Vera Atkins to author, July 3, 1949 Unaware of the radio-game, I did not at that time appreciate the significance of the remark

they resumed on June 29 they were, in the words of a report from the home wireless station, 'unusual, hesitant — quite easily the work of a flustered man doing his first transmission under protest'. However, Buckmaster and Miss Tor agreed on their knowledge of Gilbert Norman (Archambaud) that he was not the man to work under duress. By August 7, however, Antelme was able to convince them the transmissions over the Archambaud circuit showed signs of enemy control. But by August 7, it was too late to save one of the two who had just been sent over.

For what is astonishing is that despite all the warnings they had received, from Madeleine, from Cohen and from Dowlen transmitting for Déricourt, that Archambaud was under arrest, London now radioed an address, received over the Archambaud circuit, at which Bodington could meet Archambaud, at the flat of a Madame Ferdi-Filipowski in the rue de Rome. What happened next is one of the sorest points. It was Agazarian, not Bodington, who went to the rendezvous.

Vogt wrote to me that Kieffer was furious when he realised it was not Bodington but a less important man who had walked into the trap. Vogt, who interrogated Agazarian when he was brought to Avenue Foch, further wrote to me that Agazarian 'was not pleased with Bodington' for having sent him in his stead, while waiting in the neighbourhood to await the result.

I spoke to Colonel Spooner about this, but his comment was that it was better Agazarian should be arrested than Bodington, as he had less information to betray if broken under duress.

I could not see why either of them should have gone to the rendezvous. Surely it would have been better to decline the meeting-places offered, within a flat, which could be used as an ambush, and propose one in the middle of a large field, so that it would be possible to see from a long way away whether there was anybody but Archambaud on the landscape.

'Yes, yes, of course,' said Spooner. 'If that had been possible to arrange. But assuming that for some reason one of them had to go into that flat, militarily it was better it should be the less important man.'

Déricourt always put it not that Bodington had sent Agazarian in his place but that Bodington not thinking it good to go, Agazarian's undertaking to go in his place was not stopped by him.

Déricourt's own position was critical. He knew Archambaud was in German hands and that whoever went to that rendezvous would be arrested. But he had warned once by radio, and did not want to have to explain in plain language it was from the Gestapo he knew. Bodington, Déricourt told me, had belonged to the same set as himself during the war. Bodington was an enthusiast of dirt-track racing, which interested Déricourt, and it was through that they had met. They had both taken drinks in Boemelburg's flat. Meeting again in SOE, they had neither of them commented upon the fact that they had met earlier, in German company. But he did not think it could be far from Bodington's mind that he might have made contact again with Boemelburg, and he had let drop some flagrant hints he was under Gestapo protection. Bodington would, therefore, sense subtle warning intimations in Déricourt's words which Agazarian would not heed.

Also, if neither Bodington nor Agazarian walked into that ambush, Déricourt was going to have to explain to Boemelburg how they had both cried off. I am willing to believe he did try to dissuade Agazarian from going to the rue de Rome, short of explaining the whole situation. Yet if

Agazarian was willing to go, it was providential and he was not stopped.

The arrest of Agazarian was certainly the one that Déricourt felt the most heavily, for he had worked with him and liked him. He spoke of it as if it were a fatality; a heavy thing, inevitable in the circumstances.

Another part of Bodington's mission was to contact Frager. This, because of Frager's connection — knowing or unknowing — with the German Abwehr, through Bardet and Bleicher, was perilous. In Déricourt's words to me, if Bardet was brought into it, 'we were all dead'. It was because of that, he told me, that they employed Simone (Vera Leigh) as cut-out, to arrange an outside place at which Bodington and Frager could meet, without Frager's learning where Bodington was being lodged. Even so, Déricourt told me, it was through that, that Bleicher learned Bodington was in Paris. Frager took the occasion of the meeting with Bodington to tell him he had been most reliably informed, by a pro-British German, Colonel Henri [Bleicher] that Gilbert [Déricourt], 'the man who does the pick-up. operations' was a Gestapo agent. Bodington, lodged by Déricourt sometimes in Claire's and (when Bleicher was out of the way) sometimes in Déricourt's own flat, was not impressed.

Bleicher was after the war to claim that he could have arrested Bodington, had he wished, but decided against it as London would only have replaced him by a better man.

Déricourt dismissed this pretension with an indignant, 'That was the fox saying the grapes were sour, because he could not get them!' (Déricourt was always reading the Fables of La Fontaine, and drew much imagery from them.)

In any case, there must be something wrong with the conversation between Kieffer and Bleicher as related in Bleicher's memoirs:[52]

> Kieffer of the SD rang me up.
> 'Do you know that Bodington is in Paris?'
> I appeared surprised.
> 'The things you tell me, Kieffer. So what?'

Déricourt asked me, 'Did you ever hear a Sergeant answer back to a Major?'

Vogt, also, objected that it was impossible Bleicher should ever have spoken to Kieffer, in reality, as he made himself do in his memoirs, because of the difference in rank. Vogt, in parenthesis, was Untersturmführer, second lieutenant, and went in at that rank. There is, indeed, some mystery as to why Bleicher, despite his signal successes, never obtained a commission, but it seems not impossible that the tendency to build himself up to more than life-size which has been so notable in his post-war writings had begun to show while he was still in the service and decided his superiors to keep him back. Perhaps, as Christmann said, 'His pseudonym went to his head.'

In any case, the boast that he could have learned from Roger Bardet the address of Bodington and so brought about his arrest, though a high-spot in his memoirs for public consumption, does not figure in his deposition for the DST, which had only this to say about it:

> I gave Frager a second very pressing warning in the course of
> an interview which I asked him for after Sturmbannführer

---

[52] *Colonel Henri's Story* [memoirs of Sergeant Bleicher], translated and edited by Ian Colvin (Kimber, 1954), p 124.

Kieffer had apprised me of Major Bodington's arrival and that Gilbert had immediately notified the BDS. Stbf Kieffer, being ignorant of his domicile, had telephoned to me to ask me to come to his office. There he told me that he knew from Gilbert that Bodington had already arrived and wished at all costs to arrest him; he asked me whether by any chance I knew anything about it and if by any chance I knew his address.

To avoid that arrest, Stbf Kieffer insisting on it and declaring that if needs be he would not hesitate to arrest Claire, the radio operator of Gilbert, to obtain the address, I saw Frager a second time, revealing the facts to him and begging him to warn Bodington to change his address. Frager told me later that he had done this, but that neither Bodington nor the British service had taken heed of the warning.

I think one must view sceptically Bleicher's claim to have been trying to prevent the arrest of Bodington, his chiefs being set on it. He would hardly have dared to defy them on a matter of policy, and that he was certainly not secretly pro-British can be seen from the enormous number of arrests he made. Considering how unmercifully he bamboozled his prisoners — for instance the unhappy Marsac — I have been surprised by the extent to which post-war writers have seemed disposed to accord oracular status to Bleicher's narrations.

Déricourt played a good deal (hopefully) with the idea that Bleicher was in part confusing him with Archambaud — the two Gilberts. I do not, for the main part, feel that this is so, his gunning for Déricourt being so insistent. Yet it is true that Kieffer would have known of Bodington's presence in France through Gilbert-Archambaud, in the sense of over Archambaud's radio-set. Also, Claire was not a radio-operator; Déricourt suggested Bleicher confused Claire with Madeleine, who was at one moment living in Claire's flat. And I would think Bleicher meant Madeleine, who was Déricourt's radio operator at that time.

In fact, Bodington, having lost Agazarian, was now without a radio-operator of his own and so had resort to Madeleine. It must have been she who sent and received the messages between him and London by which his return flight was arranged.

For the last week of Bodington's stay, Déricourt put him into the house Jean Besnard had rented for Claire and as a safe-house for the service, at Yerres, Seine-et-Marne. It was there, while they were staying under the same roof, that Déricourt had more conversation with Bodington. It was here that he told Bodington he had 'met old friends again'. So he put it to me, making the point that he did not spell the situation out in black and white, as he did not want to put Bodington under an obligation to tell Buckmaster on his return to London. Bodington and Buckmaster were then still of the same rank, Major, and he, had hopes Bodington might take over.

Before he left, Bodington authorised the purchase of a small café near the Place St. Michel to be run by Claire as cover for a letterbox and rendezvous for agents seeking to escape, from all parts of France, by Déricourt's aircraft. Marc told me in 1943 he had suggested it should be a bookshop, 'less obvious than a café and one could exchange messages while pretending to browse among the books'.

If Bodington had understood that Déricourt was Working under the protection of Boemelburg, it is strange that he should have taken this step to extend the sphere of his operations. Or perhaps if he had grasped the principle that passengers leaving France by Déricourt's aircraft were absolutely safe, it seemed to him apt to exploit the situation to the full and get as many people out as possible by the protected line. Vogt's statement for me mentions that Kieffer's service came to know of Claire's café, which served as a letterbox. But it is possible Déricourt took care that the mail exchanged through Claire's café contained nothing of too great importance, or that he sifted it before handing over to Boemelburg what he thought fit. It may also be that the establishment of the café was something of which, when talking to Boemelburg, he could make a great deal — sufficient to induce Boemelburg to abandon the idea of trying to capture Bodington. For certainly Boemelburg must in the end have agreed that Bodington should not be arrested, and as there must have been a very substantial sop to offer him for letting Bodington go it may have seemed news of a café-letterbox would be the most harmless kind of sop; and in truth I do not know of any harm that came to the French Section through Claire's café.

On the night of August 15/16, Bodington was boarded on a Lysander aircraft, together with Lise and Claude de Baissac, and seen off by Déricourt and Marc from the field by Pont-de-Braye — which Marc, thirty years later, drove me to see.

Shortly after his return to London, Bodington left SOE for six months to lecture on French politics to troops. Déricourt suspected he had been unofficially 'sacked', but I have no information about this.

By the August moon also, four days after he had seen off Bodington, Déricourt conducted another operation, in the Angers district, on the field at Soucelles, on the night of August 19/20. This time it was an unusually large party that was leaving, ten passengers. One of these was Francis Basin (Olive) the former chief of the SOE network on the Riviera in the days of *Carte*. After a year in prison, since his arrest, he had managed to escape. Somebody told him that there was a secret regular air-service to Britain run by Gilbert, and gave him the means to contact him. Although the contact had not been given him through London, Déricourt admitted to being the Gilbert who ran the air-service and agreed to take Basin under his wing, as it was an emergency. Normally, he boarded only passengers whose code-names had been radioed to him by London, but he supposed London would want one of their men back 'from the dead, almost', and it was a humanitarian act. He added Basin to the party on his own responsibility. The others to go included Robert Benoist, Vic Gerson, A. Brooke, R. Boitreux, O. Simon, J. Marchand, J. Regnier and Marie-Thérèse le Chêne.

One of these, Boitreux, was after his return to London to make somewhat unflattering note of the arrangements in his report, and the same appears in his book,[53] where he complains of the number of passengers travelling by one aircraft, the presence of cows and horses on the field and the non-appearance of Déricourt and Marc until about half an hour before the operation.

I feel that this is somewhat unfair. First of all, the number of passengers to be boarded was decreed by London, not by Déricourt. London ordered him to fetch and board nine. By accepting Basin he added one more, but to have left him to be recaptured by the Gestapo would have been inhuman.

The complaint about livestock also seems to me unfair. SOE had no airfields of its own. In enemy occupied territory, Déricourt and Marc could only use farmers' fields, and for obvious reasons it was impractical to tell the farmer they were

---

[53] *Watch for Me by Moonlight* by Evelyn Le Chêne (Eyre Methuen, 1972)

arranging for a British secret aircraft to come down on his land and ask him to keep it clear. Fields not used for growing crops are normally used for grazing livestock. As it would not be possible to land an aircraft in a field of tall growing corn, the air operations did usually take place on fields with cows. One was lucky if there was not a bull. On the day Marc showed me the field at Soucelles, there was a bull, as well as cows and horses. Déricourt and he always sent the beasts back, by walking towards them, spreading out their hands and making shooing noises. In any case, when the aircraft began to descend, the animals would be alarmed by the noise of the engine and all run away. They never had one charge or get under an aircraft.

On the other hand, when I talked to Group-Captain Hugh Verity about this, he made the point that, even if it was only a horse, 'to a pilot, about to take off in a mist, using instruments, it is alarming to be told to look out for *anything.*'

Déricourt and Marc normally took a train earlier than their passengers, so as to arrive at the nearest railway station at midday to inspect the field leisurely and make sure there was nothing untoward — such as a heap of agricultural instruments in the middle, which unless removed could overturn an aircraft. Later they would go back to the railway station to meet their passengers and give them their bicycles and detailed instructions for finding the assembly-point, which they would reach separately. Marc showed me the assembly-point at Soucelles, a tiny bay in a hedge inside an uphill field facing the flat field on which the operation would take place. These two fields were separated by a small road, and Déricourt and Marc would wait in a room they had taken in one of the cottages on that small road. About half an hour before the operations they would leave the cottage, collect the passengers from the assembly-point and lead them across the road and down the bank to the operation-field.

As a matter of fact, Déricourt had all that day been unwell, and on their way back from the field, on the small path leading from it to the road, he fainted. Unusually, they were alone as they retraced their steps, the solitary incoming passenger, carrying a case said to contain explosives, had walked straight off without waiting for them. Marc helped Déricourt to a tree — which he showed me — against the trunk of which he propped him, until he was sufficiently recovered to be helped back to the cottage.

Shortly after this, Marc had to take something to the mother-in-law of Hercule, Madame Menon, at her school. While he was there, Germans came in and arrested the whole school. Nobody knew why, and after a little while they were all released. Nevertheless, as it was a rule of SOE that anyone who had passed through German hands, however, briefly, should report to his chief and go to England for clearance, he reported at once to Déricourt, who arranged to have him flown to England by the next aircraft.

On September 17/18, they received two Lysanders on the gently sloping field near Le Vieux Briollay. The passengers alighting were Yolande Beekman ('Mariette'), Harry Peulevé, H.M.R. Despaigne and an RF agent, H. d'Erainger ('Toinot').

The outgoing passengers included one very important man, General Zeller; the others were Benjamin Cowburn, John Goldsmith, André Renan, chief of a Polish network, and another Pole, and Marc.

Peulevé was destined to work for seven months in the mountainous Corèse district of central France and was only arrested through a local denunciation. Yolande Beekman went to St. Quentin as radio operator to Guy Bieler — but St. Quentin was in the heart of Placke's area.

This is a story with many threads to follow, and we have not yet noticed what happened in consequence of the arrest of the two Canadians, Pickersgill (Bertrand) and Macalister (Valentin). Pickersgill had been supposed to take over an area in the north, covering the departments of Nord, Aisne and Ardennes, with Macalister as his radio operator. Naturally, this was organised on their behalf by Kieffer's department; one Holdorf impersonated Bertrand, while Placke, posing as a friend from Paris, was the real chief. Messages concerning parachute operations were exchanged with London over the Valentin circuit, and a succession of parachuted cargoes were received on fields in this area by French agents of the Avenue Foch and taken into German custody. This was destined to be the longest running of the North Pole type operations in France. Neither were its evil consequences limited to the north.

London now sent an instruction to Bertrand over the Valentin circuit that he should go to the Café Colisée on the Champs Elysées, Paris, and ask the cloakroom attendant in the basement for Mlle. Madeleine. Simultaneously, London sent a radio instruction to Madeleine to present herself at the Café Colisée and asked the cloakroom attendant in the basement for Bertrand; naturally, Placke and Holdorf kept the appointment in the names of the two Canadians, Bertrand and Valentin, and that was how Madeleine found herself in contact with two Germans, who spoke French well enough to deceive a girl who was half Indian and half American. Unsuspecting, she left the café with them, and introduced them to members of the Resistance with whom she was in contact with regard to work in the north, including the director of an iron foundry and a certain Gieules, who when I saw him, in 1949, was furious about having been introduced by Madeleine to two 'Canadians' who were Germans, in consequence of which he was later arrested and spent the rest of the war in Buchenwald. Bodington, he declared was a *saland*, a man who had not done his duty. Madeleine had told him Bodington was coming from London and would meet him, then that Bodington had already returned to London, without finding time to meet him. Bodington had been sent from London to find out whether everything was all right, and had returned to England without discovering the 'Canadian' network was run by Germans.

This may have been unfair to Bodington, for I do not know whether he had instructions to check upon the authenticity of the Canadian network. With all that Déricourt told him — or did not tell him — obliquely or otherwise, Bodington had probably too much on his mind to be able to think of anything else.

VIII: THE BAD AUTUMN

Madeleine's reports from the field, some personal letters including one to her mother, which she sent by a homeward-bound aircraft, and a report by a M. Andrès concerning the effects of the RAF bombing of Courbevoie, in September, which was given her by Madame Aigrain, and which she gave to Déricourt to add to the mail, all found their way to the Avenue Foch in photocopy. This must have been Déricourt's doing. It must be appreciated that the Andras report and Madeleine's letter to her mother contained no information which, falling into the hands of the enemy, mattered. The photocopies were useful only on the plane of psychological warfare, that is, to show to prisoners in order to create dismay. It may have been the same with Madeleine's own reports. There is no evidence that Déricourt intended her any personal harm.

Déricourt told me Madeleine was extremely upset following a burglary at the flat in the rue Berlioz, which belonged to Claire but where she was staying in Claire's absence. Although all the drawers were pulled out and the contents thrown about, she realised it was not thieves but the Gestapo that had been at work. Vogt told me Kieffer sent some men to Claire's flat with instructions to pull drawers out and throw things about as if the place had been ransacked by thieves, but he could not remember, if he had ever known, what was the object of this exercise. Anyway, Madeleine moved once more; and after an attempt to trap her on the Avenue Mac-Mahon, consequential on the Café Colisée, knew herself hunted. Two of Gieules's colleagues, Arrighi and Vaudevire, refused to work longer with her, as they were sure she was followed.

Early in October, Madeleine was telling all her friends she was returning to England. To Raymonde Prénat she gave a gold powder-compact as a parting-gift. She told Madame Jourdan that on October 14 she would meet the person who would tell her where she should go to meet the aircraft. On October 10 she went to say good-bye to Madame Aigrain and told her, too, that she would be

leaving on October 14. (On October 11, the Gestapo arrived *chez* Madame Aigrain, where they arrested her and Andrès.)

The story of the arrest of Madeleine is fully related in my book on her;[54] briefly, it was a private denunciation, motivated by jealousy, by a woman, Renée, who rang the Avenue Foch. Kieffer detailed Vogt to deal with this woman, who first let him into the flat where Madeleine was staying, and showed him her radio-set and the drawer in which she kept a complete set of all the back messages exchanged between herself and London since she arrived in the field. A colleague had asked her to destroy these, but she insisted her instructions from London were to preserve them. Miss Atkins has asked me to make plain that the instructions were, on the contrary, to destroy them; nevertheless Professor Foot found instructions to another radio operator to be 'extremely careful with the filing of your messages'. Apparently, this was intended to mean only that they should be given sequential numbering. However, Vogt found all Madeleine's decoded messages filed, in the

------

[54] *Madeleine* (Gollancz, 1952), now re-issued in expanded form as *Noor-un-Nisa Inayat Khan GC Madeleine* (East-West, Rotterdam, 1971, now distributed in this country by Fine Books, 115 Bayham St, London, NW1)

more ordinary sense, and it was these that, when studied alongside of her recorded transmissions, revealed her code.

Vogt installed Pierre Cartaud to lie in wait for Madeleine and return to the Avenue Foch. Later in the morning, of October 13, Kieffer told him Cartaud had telephoned to say she was so wild he was unable to place the handcuffs on her; Kieffer told Vogt to go to his assistance, taking a party of SS. When he re-entered the flat, he told me, the spectacle which met his gaze was one of the funniest he had ever seen. Cartaud was cringing away from her, against the furthest wall, holding her away with his revolver, while she faced him with her fingers arched. 'Pierre was afraid for his eyes. She was like a tiger.' He took her back to Avenue Foch, where she made her first attempt to escape within half an hour. During the five weeks that he was her interrogator, with sole charge of her case, she was steadfast in her refusal to betray her colleagues. 'I suppose she was the best human being I have met,' he said to me.

She did, however, ask Vogt for a change of clothing and some effects she had left behind at the flat; he told her to write a note to Solange, to whom the flat belonged, requesting her to give these things to bearer; and he gave the note to Cartaud to take round. Cartaud came back, almost beside himself with excitement, to say, 'Phono is there, with his wife.'

Vogt knew that 'Phono' was the code-name now being used by Garry, and went with a party to make the arrest.

Madame Garry told me they had gone there the previous evening, October 17, hoping to pick up a message telling Garry where he should go for his flight to England, which he had understood would be between October 20 and 25. When Cartaud came with the letter from Solange, on the morning of October 18, they thought he was an Englishman — he offered English cigarettes, which he said had been delivered by parachute — and so did not hurry over their breakfast, and were still there when he came back with Vogt and the SS.

Madame Garry told me that although Cartaud was French, it was he whom she felt frightened of, rather than Vogt. 'Cartaud was young and liked to show his strength and I was afraid he might hurt us if we were left alone with him.' On the other hand, Vogt 'treated us as the enemies of his country, but with humanity.'

Miss Atkins told me Madeleine never asked to be brought back and that no arrangements were made to bring her. Yet I cannot help feeling that they were intended; otherwise how could she have conceived such a false idea in such precise terms? Déricourt told me he received no instructions from London to board either Madeleine or Garry. There were two flights which left by the October moon, one from Pocé-sur-Cisse on October 16/17 and the other from Soucelles on October 20/21. If a passenger had been instructed to meet him on October 14, it would have been for him to tell her to go to the Pocé field, for the former; and if a passenger had been expecting a contact with him on October 18, it would have been to receive instructions for the Soucelles flight. The operation at Pocé brought back Marc (Rémy Clément) together with 'Geoffroi' (Art Watt), to be Déricourt's radio operator, a triumph for Marc's insistence that Déricourt must be given a radio operator of his own. The passengers leaving France were Hector (Maurice Southgate) and 'Micky' (R. Dumunt-Guillemet). If all passengers were not aboard who should have been, why, he asked, did he not receive a reprimand from London?

London radioed Déricourt instructions to board four passengers on the aircraft that would leave from the field at

Soucelles on the night of October 20/21. As usual, the rendezvous was included in the radio-instructions, together with the pass-phrases by which he and his passenger should identify themselves to one another. At one of the rendezvous, the person who presented himself and spoke the correct pass-phrase was Roger Bardet. As Déricourt regarded Bardet as hostile to himself, he was delighted to think that he would have the duty of shepherding him out of France.

As usual, Déricourt and Marc went down to Angers by an earlier train, to inspect the field. In the early evening, they went back to Angers station, to meet their four passengers, who should be sitting in separate carriages on the later train, and give them the bicycles they had just got out of the *consigne*. Instructions were then given the passengers that dinner would first be taken, at a restaurant just across the square from the railway station, after which the members of the party would make their way separately to the assembly-point, particulars of which would be given them.

As they were crossing the square, it was noticed that Roger Bardet was lagging behind the rest of the party. Déricourt, suspicious, went back to see what he was up to, and saw that Bardet was being followed by Frager — and that Bardet, indeed, was hanging back in order to make it easy for Frager to follow. Déricourt walked straight up to Frager and upbraided him for stalking one of his operations. Frager then said it was he who was to depart by this air-operation; Bardet was merely standing-in for him.

Déricourt was furious. He told Frager he had no right to have told the secret pass-phrase to another person, however close to him. How did he, Déricourt, know, in any case, that it was Frager, as it was said now, and not Bardet, who was supposed to go?

There was a violent exchange of words.

Marc had looked round to see what was happening to Déricourt, and began to walk back to join the three, and heard some of the row. He, too, considered Frager's conduct inexcusable. But he suggested they proceed to the restaurant and talk it out quietly over dinner.

The other passengers were Francis Nearne (a brother of the more famous Jacqueline and Eileen Nearne), N. Leprince (a Giraudist agent) and Alexandre Levy, chief engineer of the Bridges and Roads (*Ponts et Chaussées*) section of the Public Works department of Paris. To Marc's way of thinking, it was perhaps the latter who was the most important passenger, as his special knowledge of bridges might be invaluable to the Allies, when planning their entry into Paris. Marc recollects that the engineer tried, vainly, to mediate between Déricourt and Frager, mainly in order to quieten them, as he was afraid that the raised, angry voices would attract notice.

This, incidentally, is the party which Garry, if his message from London was genuine, should have formed part of.

At table, Déricourt said that since Frager and Bardet both possessed the pass-phrase radioed from London, and he had therefore no way of knowing which one of them London wanted, they must both go.

Bardet did not want to go, and the argument continued over the meal.

Déricourt said that Frager's furtive conduct implied a distrust of himself; and Frager — who was going to London on purpose to denounce Déricourt there as a Gestapo agent — denied that this was so.

The party dispersed, after the passengers had been given instructions as to the assembly-point.

Later in the night, when Déricourt and Marc went to the bay in the hedge near the village of Soucelles, to lead their assembled flock from it to the operation-field, the matter was still in dispute.

'I tried to make Bardet board the plane,' Déricourt told me. It was not, however, practical to force him aboard, as he resisted.

Frager, having mounted the steps of the aircraft, turned round from the top of them and held out his hand to Déricourt.

'I refused it,' Déricourt told me.

Marc, when I saw him so many years after, confirmed that Déricourt refused Frager's hand. He gave Frager his own, in an attempt to make relations better. Yet in this matter he wholly supported Déricourt, even after the thirty years that had elapsed.

The passengers who had stepped down from the Hudson were Robert Benoist (Lionel), A. Browne-Bartroli (Tiburce) and J. Marchand. Browne-Bartroli was suspicious, and today attributes his survival to having slipped off on his own. On the other hand, Benoist, who had confidence in Déricourt, accomplished his mission unharmed, though so far from fleeing Déricourt he had meetings with him afterwards. Marchand became the Organiser of a successful network in the Lyons area, which continued right up until D Day and beyond.

But Frager, in London, was telling Baker Street he was convinced it was true, as he had been told by Colonel Henri [Bleicher], that Déricourt was an agent of the Gestapo.

At Baker Street, there was an understandable reluctance to take it on hearsay from a strange German calling himself Colonel Henri that the Air Movements officer, who was giving very good service, entertained treasonable relations with the enemy. Yet Frager's representations did cause some uneasiness, and Déricourt received a radio suggestion he should come to London again for consultation.

This he was reluctant to do, for a number of reasons, of which the most worthy of respect is that if he went to London and were there detained, Marc would be unsheltered.

Marc had already, at least once, been followed, in the metro. Marc told me that he was always very careful when travelling in the metro. He would notice all the other people in the compartment, so that if one of them reappeared in his vicinity later he would be aware of it; and he never went direct from one station to another without getting out of one train and into a following one. Supposing he wanted to go from Concorde to Palais-Royal, which is a short, direct journey: he would stand near to the doors and when the train stopped at the intermediate station, Tuilerie, just before it moved on again he would get out, squeezing through the opened doors just before they shut, so that it would be difficult for anyone else in the compartment to slip out in order to follow him. When the train had gone out, he would wait on the platform and take the following train, feeling reasonably certain that if somebody had trailed him from Concorde they could not predict it was to Palais-Royale he was really going. 'A nuisance — especially if one was in a hurry — but worth it, for the sake of feeling safe.' On one occasion, however, shortly after his return from his visit to London, he was horrified to see coming up the same staircase as himself, as he was leaving the station, a man who had been in the same compartment as himself on the first train.

He told Déricourt about this. It never happened again. Looking back on it with all that he knew now, he said to me in

1973, it was obvious what had happened. 'He must have said to his German chief, "Don't follow Marc; he notices!"'

Déricourt gone, Marc, and all Déricourt's team, would be exposed. Déricourt tried to put off London. If there were new instructions, could they not be radioed, to avoid the necessity of his leaving the field? London's hints became stronger. Déricourt mentioned to Marc that London was asking for him.

'It is perhaps because they want to give you a DSO,' said Marc.

When he had been in London, Morel had told him how highly Déricourt's work was appreciated, and said, 'We're putting him up for a DSO.'

Marc had not said anything about it to Déricourt, as it was supposed to be kept as a surprise, until he saw that he was nervous about going to London.

Déricourt seemed to brighten. 'Oh! Do you really think it is for that?'

Marc assured him of what Morel had said. And yet, Marc told me, even as he assured Déricourt, privately he had misgivings. Frager was in London, speaking against Déricourt...

Déricourt was privately in a quandary. If he showed himself unwilling to go to London, London would become suspicious, and the charges that Frager was making against him would acquire credibility. But if he went, and was detained, there could be reprisals against those closest to him. His wife had been all the time living in their flat in Paris and would be vulnerable. Marc, Claire and Watt would be left exposed, as well as all the lesser people whom they had drawn into cooperating with them. He could not confide in Marc, because then it would have been Marc's duty to inform London; failure to denounce would have been complicity. It was a case where

— to borrow a phrase Déricourt used to me in a different content — deception corresponded to respect.

He told the Germans he would have to go to London but that he hoped to be back, so as to give them an interest in not arresting those whom he was obliged to leave behind; and as an earnest of his intent to continue rendering service, he told them that the next aircraft from London would come on the night of November 15/16 and he would receive it on the field at Soucelles.

Boemelburg was out of Paris — in Vichy — at this moment, and the matter was therefore handled by Kieffer, who had never met Déricourt. From what he had heard of him, he did not trust him. Déricourt was not to depart for England by that particular aircraft, yet because it was nearing the end of his mission, perhaps suspect in London and perhaps ready to double-cross the Germans to rehabilitate himself with London, Kieffer was anxious lest something untoward happened, from the German point of view, and ordered that security measures, additional to those usual, should surround this last operation. Vogt, from whom I have this, had no direct part to play in the arrangements, and as one's memory of hearsay is usually less accurate than one's memory of events in which one has participated, I think he made a mistake when he said that Kieffer required — contrary to usual practice — that some of his own men should be on the field, as part of the reception committee. Nobody was ever on the field excepting Déricourt and Marc, and latterly a certain Dumesnil, whom Déricourt had taken on to assist him during the time that Marc was in London, and whom they had retained. Extra men could not therefore have been posted on the field unobserved of Marc. What one can retain from Vogt's recollection is that there were extra men posted somewhere.

Marc still remembers what happened that night with needle-sharp clarity, and gave me in addition to his verbal recollections a copy of his statement to the DST of February 10, 1947.

Déricourt and he had a large party of people — ten — to see off, one of whom was the French statesman, François Mitterand. On the field, Mitterand and one of the passengers alighting, Fille-Lambie, recognised each other and shook hands as they crossed. The arrivals were Vic Gerson ('Vic'), Captain Fille-Lambie ('Morlane') of RF, Captain James F. Menesson ('Henri'), and Lieutenants Eugène Levene ('Boniface'), Paul B. Pardi ('Philibert') and André A. Maugenet ('Benoit') — the last named not to be confused with Robert Benoist.

For security they split, one party walking with Déricourt to the small nearby station of Tiercé, the other cycling with Marc to the next small station, Ettriché, to pick up the same train, coming from Angers. At Le Mans, they all had to change trains, and Fille-Lambie parted from them, as he was going to Rennes. Déricourt and Marc had to get on to the express for Paris, with the rest of their charges. On the platform they noticed a group of men of unmistakable appearance — large men, without luggage — and when they had boarded the train, distributing themselves through several compartments for security, they noticed that these men were also on the train, and were distributed through the compartments. Déricourt and Marc warned their charges the Gestapo was aboard the train. When they arrived at the Gare Montparnasse they were amongst the last to get off; they saw some people arrested, but not those they had brought from Soucelles, and they thought their charges had passed through the barrier safely. In fact, the Bony-Lafont trailing gang had made a mistake and arrested the wrong people, but it discovered its mistake, and Menesson, Pardi and Maugenet were arrested.

Menesson and Pardi died.[55]

---

[55] Menesson was executed at Flossenburg on March 29, 1945, and Pardi is believed to have perished in the concentration camp at Ravitsch Colonel Boxshall, Foreign Office, in letter to author

IX: THE TURN OF THE YEAR

An escape route was penetrated again that autumn. On the road between Perpignan and the Pyrenees, a greengrocer's lorry was stopped by a road control and, unusually, searched thoroughly and the four hidden passengers discovered. Gerson — for this was on the *Vic* line — suspected the lorry driver of having betrayed them to the Germans, but in fact the four men were Abwehr agents belonging to Colonel Giskes. London had again been asking for some of its men back, so Giskes had had to comply and say that four of them would be sent by this route, and then set four of his own men to play their parts, and have an arrest laid on, so that the French Resistance would radio London that a misfortune had overtaken the passengers, the credit of North Pole remaining intact.

One genuine Dutch agent was, however, allowed to escape. This was one who had not been arrested on landing but placed in contact with false Resistants. When London asked for him back, Giskes decided it was a brilliant occasion to let a North Pole agent actually return to those who had sent him out. So he sent Christmann with him as a guide; this time there were to be no 'misfortunes' laid on. 'Apollo' was safely passed into Spain. Only the members of the *Vic* escape line with whom Christmann had come in contact were subsequently arrested, and so were the French people who had kindly lodged Christmann, believing him to be the Belgian guide, Arnaud.

Christmann told me — I do not know if it was another of his fancies — that he had in mind to use the occasion to obtain a flight to London, unbeknown to Colonel Giskes, but was deterred by the thought that Déricourt might report him to the SD, or even to London.

It was, he said, a few days short of his birthday, November 12, and it came to him suddenly in the night that if he approached Déricourt about that flight, that birthday might be his last.

John Starr had been parachuted on his second mission into the Jura mountains in May, 1943, with the code-name 'Bob', to organise a network in the Dijon area; his assistants were John Young ('Gabriel') radio operator, and Diana Rowden ('Paulette') courier. On July 18, he was betrayed by one Pierre Martin and arrested on the road between Dijon and Dole. During his interrogation at the SD HQ in Dijon (conducted with brutality), he was dismayed to see his interrogator had on his desk a complete list of the SOE training schools, with names of the instructors. My guess is that most of this had been provided by Déricourt. He says in his deposition for the DST that he gave the Germans all the information he had about the organisation in London and the training schools, esteeming that would be of relatively little use to them; he had not been through the training schools, but he had been much in the company of people who had. In the military sense, this information would not have been useful to the Germans, but they were able to make very good use of its psychological effect upon prisoners. Starr, seeing all that, was not the first to wonder whether somebody in the top office was not a traitor.

When he was brought up to the Avenue Foch he was surprised to see a British officer sitting in the guard-room turning the knobs of the radio to obtain music to his taste, while reading a book. This was Archambaud, who told him of the downfall of *Prosper* and of that wretched message about the double security check from London. This made Starr feel very uncertain about London. Vogt showed him a map of France on which were marked off the areas of organisers already captured, with their names, and asked him to mark off his own and to fill in his code-name, 'Bob'. His poster-artist's capitals pleased Kieffer, who asked him if he would re-copy the whole map in this style. This he did, and was then given other copying to do. Vogt assures me that as soon as he saw the file on Starr sent up from Dijon he realised the interrogators there had wasted five weeks while he spun them nothing but a fairy-story, about how he was an independent who had nothing to do with SOE at all, and that even at Avenue Foch he gave nothing away:[56]

> Bob denounced no one, no one was arrested following his arrest. Bob was one of the rare officers of the French Section whose arrest had no unpleasant consequences for his colleagues or for other agents of the French Section. Not a single paper, not a single address, was found on Bob permitting the German police to make an arrest.

Madeleine, Starr and Colonel Faye of L'Alliance now plotted to escape. In November, John Young and Diana Rowden were brought in as prisoners. Young was put in a cell with Starr for one night and told him they had been expecting a new agent, 'Benoit', to join them, and that the man who came, 'identifying' himself by handing him a letter from his (Young's) wife, who was in England, later came back with the Gestapo to arrest them. Benoit was Maugenet, one of those arrested following Déricourt's November operation at Soucelles. Elizabeth Nicholas, when searching into the fate of Diana Rowden, gleaned that Maugenet came at least as far as Lons le Saulnier with the Gestapo, where he dined and wined with them,

---

[56] Letter from Vogt to author, January 6, 1952

though a local Resistant who had been shown a photograph of Maugenet said that was not the man who came as Benoit; nevertheless, when the French Government after the war asked for the extradition of Maugenet from Canada, he disappeared to South America.[57]

As Young was a radio operator, considerable pressure had been put upon him to disclose the whereabouts of his radio-set; this he had withstood. He showed Starr his backside, which was severely discoloured where he had been beaten with a belt, being made to bend over, in the SD HQ of Lons le Saulnier.

Starr told Young of the escape plans and invited him to join in then, but Young told him he had given his word of honour to Vogt not to attempt to escape. Vogt lost sight of his prisoners after November 19.

On November 19 Vogt and Scherer were sent by Kieffer to arrest Hercule (A. Dubois).[58] As they entered a farmhouse, an enormous man rose from behind the table on which he had been actually transmitting when they came in. Unable to conceal the machine, he drew his pistol and fired, killing Scherer with the first bullet. Vogt saw his best friend fall dead at his side, and drew his own pistol. A civil auxiliary, he had been issued with this pistol when he joined Kieffer's staff and shown how to load it, also how to pull the trigger. But this was theoretical instruction. He had never been given anything at which he could aim, so as to find out whether he had really understood how to use the weapon. Now, facing across the table, the man who had killed Scherer, he pulled the trigger for

---

[57] *Death Be Not Proud*, Elizabeth Nicholas (Cresset, 1958 pp 136-37 and 147-48)

[58] Bleicher says in his deposition to the DST he was given Hercule's whereabouts in an interrogation.

the first time and fired every one of the bullets. They all hit some part of the body of Hercule. At the same time, Hercule fired into Vogt's body all the bullets that were left after killing Scherer. Vogt said to me, 'When both our pistols were empty, we stood looking at each other, across the table, weaponless, since all our bullets were in each other's bodies. Then I felt myself fainting.' When he regained consciousness, he and Hercule were in adjacent wards at the Hôpital de la Pitié, Paris. That was how it came about he was not on the scene on the night of November 25/26 when Madeleine, Starr and Faye made the attempt to escape across the roofs of the Avenue Foch which, had it succeeded, would have ranked with Casanova's escape from the Leads.

As I have told the story in detail in my books on Madeleine and on Starr, I will not repeat it here. Briefly, luck was not with them and they were recaptured.

One of the friends of Madame Balachowsky[59] was a Dr Briault, who had spent four months in Fresnes, with Placke for his interrogator. Having put it to Placke that it was merely as the owner of a house used by the Deuxième Bureau that he had become involved with it, he had been released, on an understanding he would keep Placke informed of what was going on in Vichy. The same evening, he dined with Placke and the latter's mistress Hélène Leduc. Hélène was concerned about her nine year old daughter and, evidently fearful lest an Allied victory could leave the child orphaned, said she would give all she could if Briault would assure the protection of the child after the war. On August 4, she said to Briault, 'Your English friends disgust me. We have the code and have only to

---

[59] All the details in this chapter are from Madame Balachowsky's long letter to the author of December 20, 1958

radio London and meet the parachutes on the field.' On the following day, Madame Balachowsky repeated this to Madame Monier-Vinard, so that she could let London know through the escape-line she organised via Gibraltar. She was also able to send it to London through the Swiss Intelligence service.

About the end of August or beginning of September, Briault again dined with Placke and Hélène, and Placke said to Briault, 'We have just captured a young Canadian parachutist. Poor boy, he used to be a student of philosophy in France before the war, I should like to give him books.' Briault promised him that Madame Balachowsky would bring the books to Helfene. So it was that Madame Balachowsky found herself taking books to a flat in the Square du Bois de Boulogne. (She heard from Briault that these books made Placke laugh, and declare, 'Your friend, Madame Balachowsky, has brought books of anti-Hitler philosophy!')

Madame Balachowsky's concern was to obtain better conditions of detention for her husband, and the idea arose that Placke could get him transferred from the main camp at Buchenwald to the scientific block, if as a professor he could be classified as a scientific man. At first she was in indirect contact with Placke, via Briault, and met only Hélène, but in September it was suggested she bring Professor Balachowsky's certificate of baptism to Placke at 84 Avenue Foch. This she did, and was shown up to his office on the second floor, at the back, with a window looking on to the internal courtyard. Placke offered her a cigarette, and showed her a radioset, saying, 'You see my radio-set. I communicate with London.' Nervous and bewildered, Madame Balachowsky smiled vaguely.

What was Placke's motive? Was he, already, in 1943, beginning to see the possibility of an Allied victory and trying with foresight to pave his way into the good graces of the Allies by 'leaking' information so as to be able to say he had helped them?

Madame Balachowsky saw Placke numerous times after that, though never again at the Avenue Foch. Through Placke or through Hélène, she heard a great deal of what went on at Avenue Foch. So it was that she heard of the attempted escape of Madeleine, Starr and Faye only three days after it had occurred. She had not heard of the arrest of Madeleine — indeed, not having heard this British official code-name, she did not realise that Madeleine was the young 'Jeanne-Marie' whom Archambaud had brought out to Grignon. But she now at once passed to London, through her usual channels, Madame Monier-Vinard, Vichy and the Swiss Intelligence service, the information that Madeleine, Starr and Faye had attempted to escape but had been recaptured.

Kieffer afterwards asked each of them for their word of honour not to attempt escape again. Madeleine and Faye refused and were sent to Germany in chains, to Pforzheim and Bruchsal respectively. They were later executed, Madeleine at Dachau on September 12, 1944, and Faye at Sonnenburg on January 3, 1945.

Starr gave his word to Kieffer.

Fate had sooner or later to catch up with the Elie (Sidney Jones) team. We saw them received by Déricourt when they arrived by one of his aircraft in May to liaise with Frager, who was so closely connected with the Abwehr they could be arrested practically at any time; especially as the Abwehr provided them with false papers in place of those with which they came.[60] Bastien, the wireless operator, could not

---

[60] See above

immediately start work as the timetable for his transmissions and related papers which were supposed to be on the aircraft with him in his luggage were not found, which meant that he was inactive for some weeks. When a new set arrived, Bardet supplied Bleicher with the full details and also the wavelength on which Bastien would transmit, so that the Abwehr were able to monitor his transmissions from the beginning.

Simone (Vera Leigh), the courier, was arrested by Bleicher at the Café Mas on October 30, together with an agent, 'Jocky', whom she was meeting there. The rendezvous had been betrayed to Bleicher by Bardet.

Bardet, in his statement for the DST after the war, and also in a letter to Colonel Buckmaster written while in prison awaiting trial, claimed that he warned Vera Leigh of the German intent to arrest her, but that she failed to flee and he arranged for her to be arrested by the Abwehr in order to spare her from being arrested by the SD. I do not find this credible.

Three weeks later, about November 20, Elie (Sidney Jones) was arrested at the Café Pam-Pam in the Champs Elysées, while sitting with Roger Bardet, by whom he was betrayed. The arrest was organised by Kiki (Raoul Kiffer) and the Massuy team.

Bastien had been transmitting from the house of Madame Boissard at Aulnay-sur-Bois in the Loir et Cher, where he was (without his knowledge) under the protection of the Funkabwehr; but now, without telling Bardet, in time for him to inform Bleicher, who would have protected him, Bastien began to transmit from the flat of a Madame Artus, in Boulogne-sur-Seine. The Direction-Finding cars discovered the new source of transmission, and Bastien was arrested in the flat, together with Madame Artus, her friend Balanca and —

for the sake of appearances — Bardet, the latter being of course released immediately afterwards.

Bleicher was very angry when he found that Bastien had been arrested. It had been over the Bastien radio that messages were exchanged with Frager, while he was in London. Now there was no means of learning when Frager would come back, or communicating with him.

In the circumstances, Bleicher instructed Roger Bardet to give letters to Claire, for transmission to Frager in London, via Déricourt's aircraft. Copies of these letters, he says in his statement for the DST, appeared on Kieffer's desk at the Avenue Foch.

As Bardet was a German agent, if Déricourt submitted the mail received from him to Kieffer's department, no harm could have come of it. He was simply exposing the operations of one German service to another German service.

At the end of the year, Colonel Giskes's North Pole operation in Holland was at last 'blown'.

On December 1, 1943, two Dutch agents, Dourlein and Ubbink, who had escaped from the prison at Harren, reached Spain, from which they were able to communicate with London. Because of the separation of the Sections dealing with Holland and France in London, the French Section appears not to have been made wise by the revelation that the entire Dutch Section of SOE had been run by the Germans since March 6, 1942.

Some time during the winter a decision was made that Gilbert Norman (Archambaud) should be taken from Avenue Foch, where he had been kept so long, to Fresnes. He had given parole, to Vogt, to cover only the time that they were out together. Now, as he was taken down the stairs from 84

Avenue Foch to cross the pavement to the waiting prison van, he made a sudden dash for it, running along the pavement. He was brought down by a shot in the leg.

After that, he was taken not to Fresnes but to the Hôpital de la Pitié. There he found himself a neighbour of Vogt, who was still recovering from his pistol duel with Hercule.

Vogt returned to work at the Avenue Foch in the new year, 1944, and it was at this time that a Swiss Organiser of the French Section was brought in as a prisoner, for interrogation. Like Madeleine, before him, the Swiss asked to be shot. Then he asked him if he might see Archambaud.

Vogt told the Swiss he could not allow him to speak with Archambaud alone, but that he could see him with himself present. And he took him to the Hôpital de la Pitié, and went with him into Archambaud's ward. The Swiss then told Archambaud that he had notified London of his arrest, and that a reply message had come from London YOU MUST BE MISTAKEN ARCHAMBAUD IS STILL TRANSMITTING TO US. On being shown this, he had instructed his radio operator to send a further message saying that if Archambaud was still transmitting he was a traitor, for he was certainly in German hands. Since becoming a prisoner himself, he had realised that the transmissions at Avenue Foch were done by Kieffer's staff, and therefore that Archambaud would have played no part in the use that was made of his set by the Germans. But being now a prisoner he had no longer the means to contact London to retract the calumny where it mattered. He asked forgiveness.

Archambaud said, 'Don't worry, *mon vieux*, you are certainly not the only one who has signalled me as a traitor. We shall sort it out when we get back to London after the war.'

Vogt could not remember the name of the Swiss but said he was the only Organiser of the French Section who was of Swiss nationality.

After returning to the Avenue Foch Vogt began to feel very weak, from newly healed wounds, and realised he ought not to have resumed work so soon after coming out of hospital. He told Kieffer he did not feel up to continuing the interrogation of the Swiss and asked if somebody else could take it over from him, in order to give him a few more days in which to recuperate. He believed the interrogation of the Swiss was taken over by Rühl.

Vogt told me this story during our first series of meetings in 1950. When I saw Cohen, on January 15, 1955, and he told me he had been radio-operator to a Swiss Organiser, under whose instructions he had radioed London that Archambaud had been arrested, that a reply had come YOU MUST BE MISTAKEN ARCHAMBAUD IS STILL TRANSMITTING TO US and that the Swiss, being shown this, required him to transmit that if Archambaud was still transmitting he was a traitor as he was certainly in German hands, I felt sure this was Vogt's Swiss and wrote to tell Vogt. Unfortunately Cohen had not been able to give me the name of the Swiss either, though I had wondered if this lapse of memory was diplomatic as he had mentioned the Swiss was still alive. Vogt had thought he would have been hanged in Buchenwald.

Vogt replied to me on March 23, 1955:

> I cannot remember the name of the Swiss whom I saw at the Avenue Foch towards the end of January, 1944, but I am happy to know he is still alive. When I began his interrogation he asked me first of all to have him shot within 24 hours. I tried in vain to persuade him that we would not shoot him; he was not willing to hear this and insisted absolutely on being

shot. Not being able, after his interview with Archambaud at the Hôpital de la Pitié, to continue his interrogation because of my wounds, which did not allow me to stay up for long, I lost sight of him and never heard of him further, I am the more happy to learn he is still alive.

When at the end of the year I met Madame Guépin, the *Liquidatrice* of *Prospers* affairs, she gave me both the name and the address of the Swiss, Jacques Weil, who had been Cohen's chief. I wrote to him from England, saying, 'I first heard of you from Ernst Vogt, the German who interrogated you at Avenue Foch.' I told him the story Vogt had told me about his interview with Archambaud at the Hôpital de la Pitié, and the conversation as reported by Vogt, and said I should like to see him to talk about it. He replied saying he would willingly see me when I came again to Paris; then telegraphed that he was coming to England and would call on me, which he did, with a friend. I practically greeted him with, 'Vogt asks me to give you his regards and say he is glad to hear you are alive. He had thought you would have been hanged in Buchenwald.' To this he made no rejoinder, other than, 'I could easily have been.' We talked about I forget what, over the first cups of coffee I made them. They had finished them, and I was bringing second cups of coffee from the kitchen into the sitting-room when Weil said, 'I was never arrested.' Devastated, I asked, 'Then you never met Vogt?' To this he returned no reply.

He avowed the exchange of signals with London as reported to me first by Vogt and then by Cohen, but not the conversation with Archambaud in the Hôpital de la Pitié, which he said could not have taken place as he had never been a prisoner. I did not understand why, if he was not the Swiss of Vogt's story, he had not said that when answering my first letter or when he first came into the room and I gave him

Vogt's message. I felt sure he was lying, and this embarrassed me during the rest of our conversation.

There later appeared *Pin-stripe Saboteur*, by Charles Wighton (Odhams, 1958), a story said to be of 'Robin', actually the story of Weil, to whom the code-name, status and some of the adventures of Worms had been attributed. Here it was stated that Weil left France for Switzerland in July 1943, after having seen the arrest of Worms (the real 'Robin' whom Wighton miscalls Jules.) It was, however, also stated, on p. 235 that from just before Christmas he 'shuttled to and fro across the border' and that on one of these sorties into France, in the early spring of 1944, he 'fell into German hands'. It was stated that this was at Lons le Saulnier, where the Feldgendarmerie, who detained him when he walked into a roadblock, did not realise who he was and that he bluffed them into releasing him after a few hours. Could this have been short of the truth?

It should be appreciated that nothing in Vogt's story was to his discredit. There may have been some innocent reason why he decided to keep secret that he had been brought as a prisoner to Avenue Foch. He is dead now.

X: THE RECALL OF DÉRICOURT

Bad weather during the December and January full moon periods prevented the usual air operations. Déricourt remained in Paris, waiting for instructions, and seeing Robert Benoist a few times. He received notification by radio that he was to return by the next aircraft that could be sent. This disturbed him and he prevaricated.

On the night of February 4/5 there was an operation to board a party which was somewhat large because of the suspension of operations during the two previous months. Eight passengers to be boarded included Robert Benoist ('Lionel'), P. Liewer ('Clement'), M. Lavigne ('Isabelle'), R. Maloubier, H. Borosh, Colonel Limousin and the woman who ran the restaurant used as an assembly place for Hudson parties.

The place was the vast field at Soucelles. A Hudson landed. Morel was in it, and stepped out. The wind created by the propeller whisked Morel's helmet off and Marc chased it and brought it back to him.

Morel said he had orders to bring Déricourt back, together with the passengers. Déricourt, aghast at the prospect of being taken so suddenly, without time to make any arrangement that would protect either his wife or Marc, or anyone connected with him, demurred, putting forward every excuse he could think of.

Marc, though as far as ever from understanding the true situation, was likewise appalled. 'I was dancing round them,' he told me, saying 'Don't take him away and leave me here all alone!'

He felt, he told me, a terrible fear of being left at the job if Déricourt were removed. Although he did not understand the situation, it was as if he knew by some instinct that only Déricourt's presence safeguarded him.

Déricourt said finally that he could not come that night, without having made necessary arrangements to safeguard his team before departing. If London would send another aircraft in a few days' time, he would board that.

Morel, convinced by the urgency in his voice, decided to trust him.

Robert Lyon told me Morel told him this was despite an order or instruction to shoot Déricourt should he resist the order to board the plane.

Déricourt stepped for a moment into the aircraft, to confirm that he would travel by the next one sent, and as the engines were still running, Morel could have kidnapped him.

Professor Foot writes in the official history, p. 297, 'the staff officer's judgement failed him and Déricourt remained in France.'

This comment shows Professor Foot himself failed to understand the real situation. Had Morel kidnapped Déricourt, Boemelburg, angered by his sudden departure, might have ordered the arrest of Marc, Claire and Geoffroi (Art Watt) the radio operator who had been sent out to them, not to mention all the people connected with them who performed minor services — Déricourt's wife, Marc's wife, Claire's personal friends, Dumesnil and so on. I think nobody at the London end faced the situation that if Déricourt was really in relation with the Germans, he could not be forcibly withdrawn without exposure of his team.

Déricourt could not trust Morel with the truth of a dreadful and highly complex situation, but when he said there were arrangements he must make before he could go, he was in total earnest.

Goetz after the war testified that on the evening of February 5 — that is the next evening after Morel's visit — he was at Boemelburg's home for dinner and so was Déricourt. Déricourt put it to them that he must obey the recall, otherwise he would lose all credit with London and be useless for any purpose. If he went to London, it was possible he could recover credit and be allowed to come back, perhaps even with increase of information. Now it may be that Déricourt, on this last visit, collected a payment up to date, but he had an absolute private duty to see Boemelburg that last time, tell him a story however thin which would reconcile him to his going and obtain his consent to his going. Morally, he could not go without being assured Boemelburg would not cause the arrest of the team his departure would leave exposed.

If he had been considering only his own safety, it is obvious it would have been much safer for him to go with Morel. Walking into the lion's jaws for the last time, he risked their closing on him. Had he not gone to see Boemelburg that last time, he would have let down those whom he himself had drawn into the service of SOE and whose lives depended on him.

An arrangement must have been made that he should let Goetz know when he received the final particulars. Vogt says in his statement for me:

I only saw him once, shortly before his return to London in February 1944. Kieffer had never entirely trusted him and told me to accompany Goetz to a meeting with him as a precaution, since he was afraid that Gilbert might have Goetz kidnapped and carry him off to London. The meeting took place in an empty apartment not far from the Arc de

Triomphe. Goetz had a key to it. Gilbert came alone and confirmed that he was going to London. He said he thought he was under suspicion He gave Goetz the BBC code message which would announce his arrival there. A few days afterwards we heard this message broadcast by the BBC.

The operation was from the field near Amboise, between the villages of St. Martin-le-Beau and Azay-sur-Cher. Déricourt had brought his wife with him. This Marc took hard. It looked as if Déricourt did not expect to return, and if there was room for her, why could not he be taken too? 'I am not big. I could have been squeezed in on the floor.' He noticed that Déricourt was very nervous, in a way he had not seen him to be before.

The Lysander brought two passengers, J.E. Lesage (Cosmo) and A. Beauregard. Déricourt and his wife boarded the plane, and Marc had to see it off, with the heaviest of feelings.

In retrospect, it is his having been left behind that Rémy Clément — Marc — has found hardest to forgive. What today still mystified him — now that he had known for twenty-eight years that Déricourt was in relation with the Germans — was why he had come through unscathed. 'Why did they not arrest me?'

'There's something you still don't know,' I cried. 'Déricourt looked after you after his fashion. After the fashion that was all his own. He left you in the field, but he had taken a step which insured that you would not be molested. What you don't know is that between Morel's visit and the night he left, he had been to see Boemelburg, to obtain his consent for going, and to ask him not to arrest you, as he hoped to be back.' We were standing on the field at Soucelles, over which we had watched an enormous full moon rise, as it had risen thirty years ago.

Marc was silent for some moments. Then he said in a low voice, from which the bitterness had vanished, 'The circumstances being what they were, it was the best thing he could have done.'

But in London the thought seems not to have been clear. If they got as far as to fear Déricourt had relations with the Germans, then to remove him from the field while leaving his team there was like a chess-player's thinking only of capturing one of his opponent's pieces without noticing that its removal from the board leaves a number of his own men deprived of what had been protecting them.

Had Déricourt not had the firmness to refuse to obey Morel's recall order, Marc could have had a very nasty experience. He would not necessarily have been arrested straight away but he would have been very likely to have received a visit from Dr Goetz, or somebody like that, to say, in effect: 'Your ex-chief worked for us. Now that he has left you to carry on, you had better do the same. Otherwise, we arrest you.'

Thanks solely to Déricourt's handling of the matter, he was not molested.

'But had I known then what I know today, I never would have carried on, receiving aircraft on the same grounds!' Marc exclaimed. 'Why did they send a further aircraft to me? It was not very clever.'

Déricourt, in his statement to the DST of November 1946, was careful to exonerate his team from any suspicion of complicity in his double-agency:

No one about me, that is to say in the team mentioned above, knew from me of my contacts or the game I played with the Germans. In London I informed no one of my contacts, neither while I was in France nor after I was recalled and had to furnish explanations in respect of the charges brought against me by Frager.

The atmosphere of suspicion with which I found myself surrounded made it impossible for me to give a frank account of my relations with the Germans. I should have immediately been arrested and would have paid dearly my French skin in England.

I recognise that it was my duty immediately to have informed my chiefs of my first contacts with Goetz. At the present time I do not remember clearly the reasons which determined me to put off giving an account. Later I was morally impeded by *amour propre* because of the attacks of Frager.

Déricourt had always told me that he 'lied and lied' to Wybot, and that specifically he had played up to his anglophobia, Wybot being 'a terribly intelligent being, the modern Fouqué,' but very anti-British — like de Gaulle, only more so. One appreciates therefore, that, fighting for his life, in the endeavour to get on the right side of Wybot he made the most of the unsympathetic and uncomprehending attitude in London. Yet his fears that if he 'came clean' he could be charged may have been very real. And this, if it got back to Boemelburg, could have-sealed the fate of Marc, Claire and Watt, for there would, from Boemelburg's point of view, have been no reason to grant them continued immunity to carry on an activity to which they did not make the Germans party, if Déricourt was not coming back. There is, therefore, justification for Déricourt's apprehensions as explained earlier in his statement to the DST:

I was in an impasse. If I had recounted my intrigues *in extenso*, even if I had been believed, I should have been arrested by the British authorities. My arrest could not have been hidden and would have liberated the Germans from all constraint and they would have arrested the people of whose safety my success was the sole guarantee...

As Frager's connections with the Germans were not appreciated in London and he was being sent back to France, if Déricourt had been imprisoned in England, it was indeed all too probable Frager would have boasted to Bardet of his success in getting Déricourt put out of the way, and the news would have got back to the Germans.

Marc told me that when he went to London after the war, Colonel Buckmaster, with hindsight, said to him, 'What we reproach him is not so much that he worked for the Germans as that he did not tell us about it. The only thing we reproach him is that he did not tell us.'

But Déricourt did not trust Buckmaster's comprehension or believe in him. He says in his deposition for the DST:

> Arrived in London I was received very coldly by Buckmaster himself ... I saw that I was under suspicion and discreet surveillance ... If I never spoke of my contacts with Goetz, Placke and Boemelburg, it was because the atmosphere of inquisition and suspicion was not favourable to explanations...

But what was really going on in the mind of London at the time? Professor Foot found certain indications in the files exposed to him. On October 30, somebody in the security section (identified only by a symbol), had written about 'the possibility that a serious disaster may occur in the Field through the agency of this man.' And on November 1, the same security officer sent a further communication to the French Section: 'The constant tapping of couriers yields the Gestapo in the long run a far higher dividend than the arrest of a few agents engaged in sabotage or even the break up of a whole organisation which we can re-start with entirely different personnel …' To this, Buckmaster replied, 'I cannot agree... The courier which might have been seen by the enemy is of very little practical value.'

This probably refers to the Frager mail. Frager had in his report of October 2 said Bleicher told him his July mail found its way to the Gestapo — though as he was in contact with Bleicher and as his closest companion, Roger Bardet, was a direct German agent, it could hardly make much difference if it did.

I asked Group-Captain Verity when he first realised Déricourt was in contact with the Germans. He replied, 'The first I heard of it was in January 1944, when Buckmaster told me there had been allegations he was in contact with the other side. I just couldn't believe it! But since the allegations had been made, I agreed with Buckmaster that we should mount a kidnap operation to bring him back for questioning.' He added, 'It was a shock to me. I had thought of him as a friend.'

It may indeed have been because hardly anybody in London really believed the allegations that Déricourt was brought back mainly as a matter of form, without thought being taken by Buckmaster for the situation that would be created by his withdrawal if he really was a double. Perhaps it had not occurred to Buckmaster that a double agent protects his team while, but only while, he functions. Buckmaster perhaps had not a mind for that kind of chess.

Professor Foot found that on February 10, the day after Déricourt's return to England, SOE's chief security officer was writing:

> If in fact he has been working for the enemy, then he is a high-grade and extremely skilful agent and no amount of interrogation will shake him.

SOE's chief security officer had not, apparently, reflected either that their having 'kidnapped' him left Marc, Claire and Watt exposed. In fact, Déricourt had made it all right for them with his Gestapo chief before submitting to the 'kidnap', but it could not be known in London that somebody who might be 'working for the enemy' would exercise this care for his team.

General Gubbins was away at that time, and his deputy, H.N. Sporborg, the lawyer, could see no proof of Déricourt's guilt, but inclined before the opinion of security, expressed on February 14, that the case against him was 'serious enough to prevent his undertaking any further intelligence work outside this country.' The decision he should not return was taken on February 21. Morel expressed himself 'absolutely revolted' by it.

Déricourt told me he was taken on his first arrival to Stratford-on-Avon, where he was held at the Swan Hotel for interrogation. Morel had rooms in Walber Street. Morel was one of the few persons in the French Section for whom Déricourt had genuine respect. Despite that there were some difficult patches between them he always spoke to me of Morel as a man who was alert and intelligent and did his job properly. But there were too many things Déricourt could not tell, even to Morel. Except that over the question of the mail he prevaricated, saying he had not submitted it to the Germans but that if he had it would have been worth it, for the sake of the aircraft service he was able to continue, Professor Foot does not tell us what, if anything, Déricourt admitted. Probably his defence was along the lines of that he later built up when charged in France, that some Germans had come to see him … It does not appear that he made the avowal he was subsequently to make in France to the DST, that he had given away certain of the air operations.

After a few days at The Swan, Stratford-on-Avon, answering questions and writing out statements, he was, he told me, transferred to the Savoy Hotel, London. Here he was given a room at the back with a window looking across the Thames, so that he could watch the barges go by. During his detention here, he became quite attached to the sights and sounds of the river. He could go into the restaurant and order what meals he wanted, like an ordinary guest, only as he was required to stay in this luxurious hotel, he never saw the bill for anything. He was permitted to take short walks in the street, and indeed there were no restrictions placed upon his liberty save that he was not to talk to French people. Yet he had a lunch with Robert Benoist at Prunier's.

XI: LEAP YEAR DROPS

Meanwhile, London was continuing to receive messages from Madeleine's radio-set and to reply to them. Madeleine, had been sent to Germany in chains on November 26, 1943, the day after the attempted escape across the roofs.

On the night of February 7/8, 1944, four men were parachuted to reception arranged over the Madeleine radio-circuit, now enemy operated. They were all newcomers, R.E.J. Alexandre, a Frenchman who was to be Organiser of a new network, with an American, R. Byerly, to be his radio-operator; an Anglo-Frenchman, Jacques Ledouz, who was to have set up a new network near Le Mans and a Canadian, F.A. Deniset who was to be arms instructor to Garry. All were to be met by Garry, who had been arrested on October 18, 1943. The reception committee was naturally formed by the Gestapo.

The Germans immediately transmitted to London on Byerly's set, but the messages did not contain his security checks and it was rightly concluded he was in German hands. Unfortunately, the inference was not drawn that he had been dropped directly into German hands and that the Madeleine radio must be under German control.

On the night of February 29/March 1 — Leap Year's night — three more people were parachuted to a field appointed over the Madeleine radio-circuit, supposedly to work with Garry. These were Major Antelme (Antoine), with Lionel Lee and Madeleine Damerment to be his radio operator and courier.

Lee appears to have been a newcomer. Madeleine Damerment had in 1941 worked with Madame Voglicimacci on the escape route run by Harold Cole, but this was her first appearance with SOE. But Antelme was one of SOE's most experienced and valued major agents.

Vogt told me that when Antoine (Antelme) was brought to Avenue Foch he was in a terrible rage and maintained London had sent him to his death deliberately. Troubled, I asked, 'He could not have wanted to make you believe that, for some reason?' Vogt answered, 'It would not have been possible to simulate an anger so terrible.'

This is very strange. I have been told privately that Morel did have misgivings about the Madeleine circuit, which he imparted to Antelme at least to the extent of arranging with him a private security check, additional to his service security checks, which, if it did not appear in the messages received over his circuit, would convince him Antelme had been dropped to Gestapo reception; and that this private security check never did come up in the messages. Professor Foot says Antelme did not want to be dropped blind as he no longer knew a safe-house to go to and would therefore prefer reception. But if his thoughts were of this prudent order one would have thought he would have declined reception by a circuit about which Morel felt doubtful. He could have been dropped far south, to safe reception by 'Hilaire' (George Starr), or one or two others.

An English lady who knew Antelme intimately tells me he was during that last period in London deeply depressed and filled with a foreboding sense this coming mission would be his last. He felt sure he would not return from it. She thought of this as a personal depression and tried to cheer him, telling him he had done wonderfully in the past and surely would come through all right again. A young nephew of Antoine, David Antelme, when he came to London from Mauritius on a brief visit some years ago, visited me and told me that the letters received from his uncle by the family during that last period were of the utmost gloom and conveyed an almost fatalistic conviction he was going to his death.

More recently, I have received a letter from another of Antoine's nephews from Mauritius, Alain Antelme; like David, he was troubled by the mystery concerning his uncle's death; but he did not believe for a moment that his uncle was the man to go, fatalistically, to what he was certain would be his death. So the question was, why did he go?

On the same Leap Year's night, a Belgian, J.T.L. Detal, and a Frenchman, P.F. Duclos, were parachuted to a field arranged over the Leopold radio; and on March 7 Octave Simon and his radio operator, Marcel Defence, were likewise dropped to Leopold. 'Leopold' was Marcel Rousset, who had worked in a network on the fringe of *Prosper*'s in the Sarthe, and who had been arrested on September 7, 1943. Naturally, these four dropped to German reception.

The 'Canadian' network in the north had been running in the names of Bertrand and Valentin (Pickersgill and Macalister) since their capture on June 21, 1943. Over the months, a great deal in the way of parachute cargoes had been parachuted to it, and it had claimed one human victim, François Michel, dropped in the early autumn. Now, on March 2/3, 1944, it was to claim six more: two Britons, G.B. McBain and D.R. Finlayson, two Americans[61], F. Lepage and F. Lesout, a Canadian, R. Sabourin and the gallant Rabinovitch (Arnaud), who told Starr what had happened at St. Jorioz. As he was a

---

[61] The presence of Americans in this operation strikes a new note, but according to Professor Foot (Official History pp 31-32) the American OSS had been officially merged with SOE from September 1942, though they were not much in evidence before 1944

radio-operator, he would have been under the usual pressure to reveal his security check, but he did not give it. The Arnaud (Rabinovitch) radio like the Gabriel (John Young's) was never worked back by the Germans.

An eighth victim of the radio-Valentin was the Corsican, A. Defendini, who was landed by sea, with instructions to contact Sabourin (arrested on reception) at a rendezvous fixed over the Valentin radio. Naturally, Defendini found his rendezvous was with the Gestapo.

A lady, Miss Kay Moore (as she was at that time), who was friends with Pickersgill (Bertrand) in London, told me that Pickersgill and she went often with Macalister and Macalister's girl-friend to a tea-room, which they called 'the Samovar', because the people were good about letting them sit for a long time over a pot of tea, bringing jugs of fresh hot water to fill it up. At Christmas, 1943, they obtained permission to have a personal message transmitted over the Valentin radio, for Pickersgill and Valentin (Macalister) WE KEEP THE SAMOVAR BOILING. It was a way of telling them they still thought of them. The reply which came was strangely impersonal, HAPPY CHRISTMAS TO ALL. She felt very let down and depressed, as she thought did the other girl, but it never for one moment occurred to her that the reply did not come from the men who were in their thoughts. It was only when she read my book *Double Webs*, 1958, that she realised their friends had been prisoners since they parachuted and that the strangely impersonal reply came from the Gestapo. Obviously, Dr Goetz would have been perplexed by the reference to 'the Samovar', which he would have no way to understand, but as it was Christmas-time would have taken his chance on its having some reference to Christmas and replied on that note. And the two girls would hardly have mentioned to anyone at Baker Street how let down they felt...

There was a further casualty of the radio-game, this time down south and via the Americans. A young SOE agent, Jack Sinclair, was on March 6/7 parachuted from Algiers, by the American OSS, to reception by what was supposed to be the *Monk* network in the Marseilles area, but his reception committee took him straight to prison.[62] Later in the month, Charles Skepper ('Monk'), Arthur Steele, his radio operator and Eliane Plewman, his courier, were arrested, and suspicion might have fallen upon Sinclair but that their French colleagues were certain the betrayal came from a Frenchman in the locality and indeed this person was after the war convicted.

It seems that the Americans, as well as the British, were taken in by the German radio-game.

On the night of March 2/3 Robert Benoist returned to France, together with Denise Bloch (Ambroise), as his radio operator. I think the aircraft which brought them must have been received by Marc, carrying on in Déricourt's stead from one of his old fields. They went to work in Benoist's old Nantes area.

Shortly after this Claire received a fright. Two persons came to her café asking to see her but giving the password incorrectly; they said they came on behalf of Toinot, who had to escape quickly. The barman did not know this name, and, after a behind the scenes consultation with Claire, reported she was not there. A couple of days later another man came in and said he was Toinot and must have a Lysander passage quickly. Claire was convinced he was an *agent provocateur* and that the Gestapo had got wind of her café (they had known about it from the beginning but she did not know that), and, with Jean

---

[62] Official History, pp 375-76

Besnard, she fled from Paris. Watt (Geoffroi) joined them and agreed with Claire they should leave for London. All three squeezed into the next Lysander, which left on the night of April 5/6. Marc was now left alone, with no job, since he was the only one of what had been Déricourt's team left. His work was over.

Actually, Toinot was not an *agent provocateur* but an authentic RF agent, H. d'Erainger, who had somehow learned, without going through London, that Claire's café was the starting point of the Lysander line, and he and his two friends did urgently need to escape to England; but that they did, through another channel.[63]

Frager returned to France at the end of February. In view of his admitted contact with a German intelligence man — whether or not they had grasped in London that Colonel Henri was Bleicher — it is strange he should have been allowed to do so. Bleicher's deposition tells us he saw him again in March, 1944, and that Frager, still believing him to be genuinely pro-Allied, gave him his sister's address, at which he could hide himself from the time the Allies landed — for nobody doubted the Allied landing would be in '44 — until Frager could vouch for him. Frager told Bleicher he had at last been able to convince people in London that Déricourt was a German agent, and that following an interview with Buckmaster Déricourt had been imprisoned. This was incorrect, but shows how right Déricourt was to fear that if he were imprisoned in London news would get back to the Germans through Frager and Bleicher, imperilling Marc, Claire and Watt. Fortunately, by the time this news reached the Germans that Déricourt was no longer potentially useful, Claire and Watt were back in London

---

[63] Foot, *Official History*, pp 306-07

and no more aircraft were being sent to Marc, otherwise it might have gone ill with them.

Frager now put Bleicher in contact with Benouville, of the FFI, and only because the SD were at that moment side-tracked into following up something started by Christmann did Benouville escape arrest.

In London, at least one person had not been happy about the February and early March parachutings; Morel. Morel had begun to suspect the radio-game. Determining to verify whether the 'Canadian' network in the north was really Canadian or German controlled, he had a message transmitted to the Valentin radio-set saying that in May someone would fly over and would require to speak with Bertrand (Pickersgill) by S. phone (an instrument making possible conversation between a person on the ground and one in an aircraft overhead). Kieffer instantly had Pickersgill fetched from Ravitch concentration camp, but when he discovered what was required he refused absolutely. So they turned to Starr.

Since he had given his parole, the Germans had begun what was obviously designed as a softening up process.

One evening when Placke and others came in, talking about a restaurant where they had dined, Starr said, half-joking, 'Why don't you take me out to dinner?' Placke asked Kieffer, and told Starr he received the reply, 'So long as not less than five of you go with him and that you never leave him.' He was taken in a car with Placke and others to a smart restaurant where a table had been reserved for them.

I was surprised when Madame Balachowsky wrote to me that she could tell me the actual composition of the party: Placke, Starr, and the Bouillon brothers, Hélène Leduc and Briault. Starr would have been very surprised to know that one of the part at that table was a Resistant. After the dinner, Briault did not go to bed but went straight to Madame Balachowsky, calling on her at 8 am to give her a full account of the evening, and of the conversation, which had run very much on the fake 'Canadian' network in the north and the false parachute receptions organised by Placke in the Canadians' place. Madame Balachowsky sent this information to London by her three usual channels.

As Placke knew that Briault was a friend of Madame Balachowsky and had met them together, he must have realised when he included Briault in the party that a description of it was likely to be sent to London, which raises the question of which side Placke was really on, by this time.

When Starr was asked to go to a field in the north and speak over the S. phone in Pickersgill's place, it was the first big challenge, and he knew he could not do it. Yet he did not refuse outright, but temporised, saying, each time they asked him, 'I'm thinking about it,' in a way that led them to think he would, and left it to the night itself to say, 'I can't do it.'

Von Kapri took the S. phone and endeavoured to answer Morel — for it was he in the plane. His heavy Germanic accent betrayed itself at once. Morel, realising instantly that the man on the ground was German, did not speak back to him and the aircraft returned to England.

By temporising, Starr undoubtedly rendered a service, for had he refused outright as soon as the proposition was broached to him, alternative arrangements could have been made. Vogt spoke better English than Von Kapri; but he went home in the evenings if there was not an interrogation to keep him, for he lived with his wife in a flat in Paris. Placke spoke better English than Von Kapri, but must have been allowed to go to some other place on that night. With a few days' notice, arrangements could surely have been made for Kieffer's service to borrow Harold Cole, the traitor from the MI9 Escapes organisation — who shortly after this was brought to Avenue Foch, to occupy one of the prisoners' cells though he was free to go in and out of the premises.

Placke, by this time, was behaving strangely. In one of her letters to me, Madame Balachowsky wrote:[64]

> One day he [Placke] asked me to come and see him at 8 in the morning. He had been away for a while. I arrived, and found him a changed man, saddened, not the man I had known till then. He motioned me to sit down, and said, 'Madame Balachowsky, war is a horrible thing. I have just come back from Hamburg. The English bombing with phosphorus is horrible. I had to take my family to the country.' We talked about bombing, and I told him I was always horribly afraid in a raid. He told me he was expecting Briault, who would make him forget this nightmare; he said, 'He is the most amusing Frenchman whom I know.' Briault in fact dined with him, and — an astonishing thing — Placke said to him, 'Tell Madame Balachowsky to telephone me on such a day, and she will be told where I am.' I did telephone him, and in truth a person who answered the phone said, 'Mr Placke is at...; we knew through agents who belonged to the false-reception committees who worked under Placke that they were going to carry out reprisals against a maquis. I knew then in which place the reprisals were going to be carried out, and was able to forewarn the maquis. *It is unheard of, but it is true.* The telephone number of Placke was Passy 94.56.

One has the position, then, that while on the one hand Placke was doing his best to bamboozle the British by organising a fake network in the names of the two captured Canadians, and bringing back to Kieffer the cargoes

------

[64] December 20, 1958

parachuted to the fake reception committees, on the other hand he was trying not to be too successful; that is, he was trying to leak it back to the British through Madame Balachowsky that he was bamboozling them; and on this occasion he prevented a vengeful shedding of Allied blood by warning her of reprisals to be exacted against a maquis.

XII: D DAY

In May, a new and important prisoner was brought to the Avenue Foch, Squadron Leader Maurice Southgate, 'Hector', Organiser of the sizeable network in west-central France around Châteauroux. He had been arrested when, on May Day, he had gone to see his radio operator at Montluçon without looking to see if the danger signal agreed between them was in evidence. The radio-operator had been arrested and Germans were in the premises. At Avenue Foch, returning from the lavatory he saw Starr, smoking a cigarette and wearing a tie (which others were not), and Starr saw him pale. He realised his air of being at ease had given a shock to Southgate, and took an opportunity, when Southgate was placed in a cell next to his, to whistle '*God Save the King*'. Southgate later told him he had been grateful for the signal, which he had understood.

It was Vogt who told me Southgate had been very badly beaten, not at Avenue Foch but at a local station to which he had been taken before being brought up to Avenue Foch. In fact, Starr and Southgate were the only two prisoners to show him marks of physical mistreatment which he had no reason to doubt had, as they said, been administered during preliminary interrogation at provincial HQs of the SD. Southgate had been thrashed on the back, and, arriving all tense at Avenue Foch, relaxed only gradually. Eventually he confided to Vogt that with each day that passed without torture he had said to himself, 'The torture will begin tomorrow.' Only slowly had he realised it was too late for torture to serve a purpose and that there was not going to be any.

Starr was surprised when one of the guards, answering the phone, said, 'It's for you.' He wondered who could be ringing him up at Avenue Foch; it was Vogt, from a lower floor, inviting him to come down and have lunch with his 'cousin'. Southgate was not Starr's cousin, but they had known each other since boyhood as their fathers were business associates. It was Southgate who had claimed kinship. In a room opposite Kieffer's study a luncheon table was laid for four, Vogt, Southgate, Starr and Southgate's radio operator.

Vogt wrote to me:[65]

> We found a notebook written in the hand of Hector [Southgate], which had given us all the information about his important sector, we found there all his parachute grounds with the BBC messages, the names of his collaborators and the places where they worked. It was this complete notebook and other papers found at the domicile of his radio-operator, Aimé (radio-messages sent to and received by Aimé to and from London etc) which enabled us to know all about the sector of Hector and it was also because of that notebook and papers that some arrests were made in the region of Châteauroux (if I remember well) following the arrest of Hector. It was also because of this notebook and papers found in the domicile of Aimé (where Hector and Aimé were both arrested) that I undertook the journey with Hector to the Midi of France. But as already said, this journey did not give the result hoped.

In an earlier letter, Vogt had written to me (in English):[66]

> My trip with Hector to Tarbes via Limoges did not have the result I expected. He accepted to accompany me to all the

---

[65] Letter from Vogt to author, June 6, 1952
[66] Letter from Vogt to author, November 16, 1951

towns and villages where he was working, but he accepted this about three weeks after he had been arrested, and because he knew very well that all his men had been averted of his arrest by the BBC, and that they changed their domicile and their names and cover-names. The whole trip to the South of France did not allow us to make any arrest. I went with Hector alone to his former rooms in Limoges and in Tarbes, we entered his rooms like thieves, in Limoges, by the window, in Tarbes by breaking the lock of the door of his room. All what we found in his room was not of any interest to us.

[Continuing in French]

At Tarbes we found a small Philips radio which I brought back with me to Avenue Foch. But anything that could interest our service had been removed by the colleagues of Hector. He knew it and told me before we set out, but I wanted to see for myself, in the hope they might have left something interesting. I had shown Hector the BBC messages warning his collaborators of his arrest and asking them to change domicile and take precautions. It was only about 15 days after I showed him the BBC message that he agreed to accompany us to Limoges and to Tarbes, when he knew that the expedition could not do any harm to his collaborators. The journey was moreover not without danger for me, I took the risk that Hector might be recognised by one of his colleagues and that they might attack me in order to liberate him. I passed the nights alone with him in a room at Limoges and a night at Tarbes without any guard and it did not prevent me from sleeping. In the morning at about 5 o'clock Hector and I took (or rather stole) a car from the Gestapo of Tarbes, and left together in that car, which Hector was driving (I do not drive a car and I did not know Tarbes, so he could have driven me no matter where). He drove me to his domicile in Tarbes and we penetrated into his room by breaking the lock (as we had no key and did not wish the inhabitant of the house to perceive us). In his presence I went through everything in the room but I did not discover anything interesting to our department.

When telling me this story by word of mouth, Vogt did say that on the first night that he spent in a room alone with Southgate he did really ask himself if he was mad, to sleep alone in a room with a British agent who was a prisoner of his service, unhandcuffed, who might kill him while he slept, or simply get up and go away. He had, of course, obtained Southgate's word of honour before setting out on this expedition, but did not know whether the parole would hold, under the temptation of so much opportunity for escape. Kieffer had given permission for Southgate to be taken by a party; it was on his own initiative that Vogt, feeling the SS a nuisance, had shed the party and gone to the various places associated with Southgate's work with Southgate alone. He had not telephoned to Kieffer to ask his permission to dismiss the guard, and if he came back having lost the prisoner, he would face Kieffer's anger. That he was able, after several days, to come back to the Avenue Foch with Southgate greatly strengthened his confidence in an Englishman's word of honour.

And though he did not find what he hoped for, the trip was, in another way, not without fruit.

Later, Starr was shown photographs which had been taken of Southgate and Vogt in the car with the SS with whom they started out.

In May, Pierre Cartaud was shot. Vogt gave me details:[67]

Peter died following a revolver-wound which he received by mistake from a French agent of our department, before a hairdresser's and parfumerie, Vincent, in the rue Royale, Paris.

---

[67] Vogt, letter to author, October 7, 1951.

The hairdresser's daughter Gisèle served as a letter-box to a French information service working to London and Algiers. Gisèle was arrested by me after this incident. After the war she returned from concentration camp in Germany and could testify to this accident in which Peter was mortally wounded.

Cartaud was shot in the stomach. He was taken to the Hôpital de la Pitié but died after a few days. Some of the Avenue Foch staff went to see him buried, though Vogt could not remember in which cemetery.

Starr was shown photographs of the funeral. 'He was buried with German military honours!'

Also in May, on May 12, a party of eight women, brought up from Fresnes, appeared briefly in Avenue Foch. Starr recognised his former courier, Diana Rowden, and offered some chocolate round to them. Kieffer, being a non-smoker, was a chocolate-eater, and on Sunday mornings would unlock each of the cells at Avenue Foch and offer chocolate, or sometimes other sweets, except to Rabinovitch, either because he was a Jew or because he was so uncompromisingly aggressive. But that was how Starr had chocolate to give to the girls.

Actually, the party consisted of Diana Rowden ('Paulette'), Eliane Plewman ('Gaby'), Yolande Beekman ('Mariette'), Madeleine Damerment ('Martine'), Vera Leigh ('Simone'), Odette Sansom, later Churchill, ('Lise') and Sonia Olschanesky. Though none as yet could know, all except Odette were doomed to die.[68]

At this moment, their appearance at Avenue Foch prior to transport to Karlsruhe, he was a sign of the expected Invasion. Once Allied troops landed in France, prisoners could become

---

[68] The story of the seven who died is movingly told by Elizabeth Nicholas in her book *Death Be Not Proud* (Cresset, 1958)

an encumbrance. For the Avenue Foch staff to have to take them along with them in a possible retreat, would be inconvenient. Kieffer had before the war been in the Gestapo of Karlsruhe, and therefore apparently thought of that as a place were they could be kept safely without his altogether losing access to them.[69]

Colonel Giskes had sent a last mocking message to London on April Fools' Day, and Kieffer sent one on D Day, MANY THANKS LARGE DELIVERIES ARMS AND MUNITIONS HAVE GREATLY APPRECIATED GOOD TIPS REGARDING YOUR INTENTIONS AND PLANS.

Buckmaster replied the same night: SORRY YOUR PATIENCE IS EXHAUSTED AND YOUR NERVES NOT SO GOOD AS OURS GIVE US GROUND NEAR BERLIN FOR RECEPTION ORGANISER AND WT OPERATOR BUT BE SURE YOU DO NOT CLASH WITH OUR RUSSIAN FRIENDS.

I give the wording of this exchange as taken by Professor Foot from the postwar testimony of Kieffer's chief, Kopkow; but while it is unlikely Kopkow could remember the text exactly there is independent testimony for something very like it. Vogt gave it to me as including YOU HAVE LOST YOUR NERVES and something about the Russians, and Placke's deposition for the DST states:

> We sent them a last message as follows: WE THANK YOU
> FOR ALL THE ARMS YOU HAVE SENT US SIGNED

---

[69] The French sub-agents of the Prosper network, amongst whom Professor Balachowsky had already been sent to Germany, from Compiegne, on January 17, 1944, letter from Madame Balachowsky to author It was in the course of this transport that Guerne escaped from the train Madame Balachowsky arranged his passage to England, through Madame Monier-Vinard and Gibraltar

GESTAPO. Dr Goetz claimed that London counselled us, the Gestapo, to continue the work towards the East but to avoid doing it too close to Berlin because of the Russians Goetz had no reason to say that, if it was not true.

Buckmaster's joke caused perplexity of a nature that would have surprised him. Armel Guerne, basing himself on Placke's deposition, put it to me that this was support for his thesis that there was some sort of collusion between London and Avenue Foch against the Soviet Union; and the Abbé Guillaume was obviously no stranger to that theory when he asked me in a very curious voice what I made of that message to the Avenue Foch from London about the Russians. I suggested, and still believe, that there was nothing in it but a reference to the fact that as the Western Allies were attacking Germany from the West, the Russians were attacking from the east, and would be likely to reach Berlin first. It does, of course, sound more sinister in Placke's version — particularly because of the significance plainly attacked to it by him — than in the Kopkow version found by Professor Foot at the Foreign Office.

Placke, for his part, was continuing to play a very peculiar role. Madame Balachowsky's letter to me of December 20, 1958, revealing him now as a double agent, at least in the intent:

After the invasion of Normandy Placke invited Hélène and five or six adjutants of Placke whose names I forget now; there was plenty of champagne, paid for by Briault, and at one moment Briault said, 'Let us drink to the defeat of the English!' to see their reaction. Placke replied to him, 'Doctor, you take us for idiots.' I know that on that day Placke made propositions to Briault; he proposed to obtain for him a German passport and that Briault should leave for Germany

with him, with a secret radio-set. Briault wanted to accept, up
to the last minute, but his wife was against it.

It sounds as though Placke was offering Briault one of the
captured radio-sets on which to send intelligence to London.

Bleicher's agents had deserted him. Roger, Bardet and Kiki
had hidden themselves in authentic maquis, hoping the long
period during which they had informed to the Germans would
never be discovered.

From Berlin, an edict arrived that all members of the Avenue
Foch staff were to wear uniforms. Till now, they had always
worked in civilian clothes, despite their SS ranks. An enormous
consignment of uniforms arrived, appropriate to all the
different ranks. Vogt believed the idea behind this was that it
would be some kind of protection to them; perhaps the idea
was that if they were overrun by the Allied troops and so
found themselves unintentionally behind enemy lines they
could get shot as spies unless they were in their uniforms.
Then it was announced that everybody was to be
photographed, and the whole staff of 82 and 84 Avenue Foch
was assembled in front of the building, with Boemelburg and
Kieffer in the middle of the front row. Just before the shutter
clicked, the man who was next to Vogt murmured to him, 'Is
this to make sure the British can recognise us, to hang us?'

From the moment Allied armies were on the soil of France
the entire character of the Resistants' war changed. It was no
longer a secret war. The maquis came out. When history speaks
of the massive rising of the Resistance to support the Allied
armies, it was mainly not the old Resistants, few of whom
survived. Of the old stagers, in F Section by far the most
notable were the three who became Colonels. Colonel George
Starr, Hilaire, elder brother of the Starr at Avenue Foch),
whom we saw arrive by felucca in the autumn of 1942 and pass

through de Malval's to the south-west, where he organised, in Gascony, a powerful maquis, which now came out of its fastness to engage the German army in the rear.

This was what Prosper had been meant to do, what all the organisers had been meant to do. When I met him, in November 1954, at the home of his less fortunate brother, he gave the credit to the type of country in which he was operating. This was becomingly modest; but as he put it to me I saw that the life of a maquis, camped out in wild forested regions was very different from that of the secret agents living in Paris or other areas of sophisticated or industrialised character. 'It was much more difficult to infiltrate us with double agents,' he said. 'I should hate to have worked in Paris.'

Indeed, SOE's other two colonels, Heslop (Xavier) and Cammaerts (Roger) worked in the High Alps and Low Alps, respectively. The long-running Brooks (Alphonse) was in the Alpes Maritime. So one has three of these successful, long-running networks in the Alps and one at the feet of the Pyrenees. Rée, who ran a longish time, was again in high country on the northern border of Switzerland. Of longish running organisers, only one, Robert Lyon, whom we saw landed to reception by Déricourt in June 1943, worked in the region of a city, Lyons; he survived to the end. It was the networks in the areas we have been studying most closely, Paris and the highly civilised Loire valley, and the industrialised north, that were the most heavily hit. There was not much here that survived from the early days to greet D Day.

One survivor from earlier days deserves mention. Robert Benoist, coming to Paris to see his mother, who was dying, was arrested on June 18; his courier Denise Bloch, was captured the next day, in the Benoist château. Vogt told me that when Benoist was brought to the Avenue Foch it was he who interrogated him and Benoist told him that when he was in London he found that Gilbert (Déricourt) the Air Movements Officer was under suspicion there of being a German agent; he said that he had been asked his opinion and had given his testimony in his favour; but he asked Vogt, 'Was he, in fact, in relation with your department?'

Vogt said to me, 'I did not answer him.'

So Déricourt's fear that whatever happened to him in London could get back to the Germans was justified. However, by this time Claire and Watt were in London and no further aircraft were being sent to Marc, so that to molest him would have been idle vengeance, even if through Vogt and Kieffer Benoist's news got back to Boemelburg.

But the characteristic feature of these days was that all over the place new men were being dropped to organise new groups. If one looks at the table which forms Professor Foot's Appendix B, one sees at a glance that of the networks operating at the time of D Day, more than half were commenced within 1944 itself; some Organisers, such as George Millar, were dropped only in June. To compare these men with those who came in the dark years, 1941, 1942, 1943, would be wrong. The new men came with the Invasion which, to Prosper and Archambaud had seemed light-years away in terms of the dangerous waiting. I do not mean that the danger was over. The chance of being killed in fighting was probably greater in this moment when there was open fighting everywhere; but it was open, and that was the difference. They were not solitaries in a subdued land, needing to fear that every person they encountered might sell them to the Gestapo. With the Invasion of the Allied armies came the uprising of the townspeople and the village people, everywhere. Suddenly, everyone had been a Resistant all along. In France, there is a mocking term, 'Resistant de '44', used to denote those many who did nothing for the cause until it was practically won, and then climbed on to the band wagon. There was fighting, but the men from London were being treated as heroes, everywhere. Very different had been the lot of those who worked for this day in the dark days, most of whom were now languishing in prison cells or in the dreadful misery of the concentration camps. If some of them acted amiss, this at least must be remembered of all who served in the field in '41, '42, '43; they went in the dark days.

Four more of the French Section girls were caught during this last period, Violette Szabo, Eileen Nearne, Lilian Rolfe and Yvonne Baysden, but all more or less by accident. Now that the Allies were so plainly winning there were not so many people willing to betray British agents to the Germans.

On July 20 there was the attempt on Hitler's life, and as part of the attempted coup most of the Avenue Foch staff was that night arrested for a few hours by another German service. Vogt, being at home when it happened, was not arrested, but when he came to the office in the morning Kieffer told him about what had happened and said that for a while he was left entirely alone in the building.

The age of the great betrayals was practically over, but there remains one more to chronicle. Pressure was put upon Bleicher by his chiefs to arrest Frager. Bleicher went to the address of Frager's sister. Frager had told her about him, and so she was trusting, and told him she was meeting her brother that afternoon at 3 o'clock at the Duroc metro station. Bleicher went with her, and Frager, who was with his wife, came up to them. Bleicher signalled to some soldiers to arrest Frager. Afterwards, he saw him in his cell as Avenue Foch, told him that Roger Bardet had been turned round and had, for over a

year, been betraying him, and asked him not to reveal to the
SD that he (Bleicher) had told him Gilbert (Déricourt) was an
SD agent:

> We both shed tears when Frager, having at length understood
> the situation, told me he still trusted me and forgave me. I
> told him there was only one thing to do, that was to avenge
> ourselves on Roger, convinced that one of us would survive
> to do it. It was then he said, 'I beseech you, Henri, do no
> harm to Roger; I have always considered him as a brother; I
> am a Christian, and practising, and I forgive him as I forgive
> you. We will settle things after the war.' I gave him my word
> of honour to do nothing against Roger, while he promised to
> say nothing of the history of Gilbert.[70]

That a man betrayed as Frager had been betrayed by Roger
Bardet, should have been moved in such a moment solely by
desire to protect his betrayer from harm, seemed to me to be
pushing Christianity beyond easy credence.

It was Déricourt who said something quite unexpected.
'Frager was paederast.'

I cannot verify this statement. Déricourt could be fanciful,
but — about people — I have never known him invent a detail
except in the sense of what he believed to be true. Déricourt
said, 'I am not being scandalous, but if you do not know that
about Frager you do not understand the story.'

Frager was the enemy of Déricourt, so it may be thought that
Déricourt would seek to damage him. Yet when I posted him a
newspaper article in which it was stated Frager betrayed
Agazarian, he replied (in his broken English),[71] 'No, the arrest

---

[70] Bleicher's official deposition to the DST
[71] Déricourt, letter to author, March 27, 1960

of Agazarian was not the fault of Frager — in spite of I dislike him.'

Déricourt was not, therefore, prepared to jump on any bandwagon, regardless of truth, in order to damage the repute of Frager, and his fairness to him makes me the more disposed to accept his good faith when he insisted to me, both in our conversations and, subsequently, in writing, that Frager was homosexual.[72]

He was Alsatian and had had during 1914/18 war a wound that had forbid him to have any children. So he was in the same mood that your 'big Lawrence of Arabia' — slight voice — no strength — complexes, and I will say a tendency to associate with young, pretty men.

I would not be sure about the detail concerning the wound, which could have been thrown in as an excuse, but, as I have said before, Déricourt does not invent details except in the sense of what he believes to be true.

If Frager was passionately attached to his betrayer, it illuminates not only that strange emotional scene but much which is obscure. To Déricourt, particularly, it explained the long blindness as to Roger Bardet's treason. For even granting that Frager was naive, trusting, unobservant, there must, over the months, have been things he saw that should have told him his friend was in the German service. Déricourt said 'He did not see, because he did not want to see ...'

In his deposition for the DST Bleicher is obviously trying to curry favour with the French by making out that he was genuinely anxious to help the Allies. Déricourt, pouring scorn on this pretension, sent me a list of the Allied agents arrested by or through Bleicher, certainly not a complete list, the names

---

[72] Déricourt, letter to author, September 26, 1958

being jotted as they came to his mind. A few of the names are unknown to me, yet in so far as I can judge it, it seems to me sound:[73]

May, 1941
Lemeur
Kiffer, Raoul — "Kiki"
Mme. Buffet
Mlle. Charlotte
Mlle. Gribault
Mlle. Grenault, Paule
Herbert
Lebeau
Mme. Auguste
Englishman shot Nov. 41

18 Nov., 1941 and following days
Christian (Bernard Krutki)
Borni, Renée
Czerniawski
M. Carré (the *Cat*)
Claude Jouffret
Ronne
Le Guillec, Madeleine
Roussel, Henri
Passenger
Koslowski
Lipski
Lipski, Lydia
Lebordais, Suzanne
De Chiahoudot, Liliane

---

[73] The list is handwritten, and I am not sure that I can read his writing (as I have indicated by question marks against a small number of unfamiliar names) I cannot check on all of the dates I have omitted Déricourt's 'denounced by' column

Godin, Fernandez
Godet, Gisèle
Honski, Wanda
Rocquiguy, Lucienne
Hugentobler
Mme. Hugentobler
Goubou, Robert
Lecourt, A.
Collardet
Sulford, Bertrand
Le Chatlier
Durbot

4/6 February, 1942
Le Tac, Yves
X…
K… (Amiens)

20 April '42
Agent of de Vomécourt

21 April '42
Volters
Roger Cottin

25 April, '42
De Vomécourt, Pierre

1 May, '42
Duprey [?], Antoine
Bandeyron, Noel
Abbott, Georges
Finken, Jacques
Redding, Claude
Henriot, Cecile
M. Goutte, Marthe

Gesnier, Felix
Besnier, Maurice
'De Jonckes, Léon
Chataigner, Sylvanie
Ambrosini, Lucien
Herin, Jules
Berstein, Daniel

25 March, 1943
Marsac
Fromageot, Lucienne

13 April, '43
Castelli

15 April, '43
Bardet, Roger
Mme. Marsac
Lejeune, Mireille
Lejeune, Henri

17 April, '43
Churchill, Peter
Lise (Odette)

24 April, '43
Tambour, Annette
Tambour, Germaine

End April, '43
Spacry

May, '43
Sajet
Dujardin

July or August, '43
Dufresnes, Jacques (Parker)

End July, '43
Lejeune, Maurice
Lejeune, Madeleine
Lejeune

Oct, '43
Simone (Vera Leigh)
Capron
Bloch

Nov. '43
Froment
Nollent
De Maistre
Dr Hautechaud
Orange
Grignole
Guilman

19 Nov. '43
Bastien (Marcel Clech)
Balanca
Artus
Hercule (A. Dubois)

20 Nov. '43
Elie (Sydney Jones)
Mme. Jones
Mlle. de Neuville

21 Nov. '43
Lemoine, Georges
Eon

Hiver

30 Nov. '43
Hewitt

Dec. '43
Haleoicq (?)
Mme.
Son
Two daughters

Jan. '44
Mme. Maublanc

End '44
Elster (2nd arrest)

Déricourt has forgotten to include Frager; but were I to insert the name I should hesitate as to the date. Professor Foot gives August 8,[74] which cannot be right (see below following paragraph); Cookridge gives July 2,[75] probably oral from Bleicher; Ian Colvin gives July 22,[76] from Jacques Adam, who took over the command of what had been Frager's Maquis on the next day. I would expect the latter's memory to be the more reliable, as the assumption of command would be of importance in his life; but Bleicher in his deposition says the arrest of Frager was on a Sunday, which the 2 is and the 22 is not (it is a Saturday). I should think the arrest of Frager took place either on July 2 or July 23.

---

[74] Official history, p 411

[75] *Inside SOE*, E H Cookridge (Barker, 1966), p 370

[76] *Colonel Henri's Story* [Bleicher's] ed Ian Colvin (Kimber, 1954), p 139n

On August 8, a large party of prisoners left Compifegne by train for Germany. The unhappy (amongst whom several names will be recognised) were Yeo-Thomas, Southgate, Robert Benoist, Culioli, Frager, Kane, Mayer, Wilkinson, Peulevé, Hubble, Barrett, Steele, Pickersgill, Macalister, McKenzie, Allard, Defendini, Detal, Leccia, Garry, Garel, Geelen, Rechenmann, Corbusier, Chaignot, Gerard, Loison, Mulsant, de Seguier, Vellaud, Guilot, Evesque, Avallard, Rambaud, Hessel and two others;[77] and, in a separate compartment, three girls, Violette Szabo, Lilian Rolfe and Denise Bloch, perhaps with other girls, not of the French Section. At one moment, two of the girls, handcuffed together, came along the corridor to offer to the men sips from a jug of water. Peulevé recognised one of them as Violette Szabo, whom he had known in London and with whom he was in love. The men were all destined to Buchenwald, Yeo-Thomas, Peulevé and Hessel later escaped, thanks to Professor Balachowsky who used his position as a man of science (gained for him by Placke) to enable them to exchange identities with three men who had died of typhus. All the rest were hanged, except for Southgate and Culioli. The three girls were sent to Ravensbruck; all were eventually shot.

John Starr was also sent to Germany. Rühl said, to him, 'Now that you're going, there's something you ought to know. Kieffer three times received an order from Berlin to have you shot, and each time he refused to comply with it.' Kieffer told Starr he was having him sent to Buchenwald, and he went direct from Paris, in a train carrying otherwise only French and East European prisoners. The train stopped at the station for Buchenwald but word got round that the Camp Commandant

---

[77] *The White Rabbit*, Bruce Marshall (Evans, 1952), the names from memory of Yeo-Thomas, p 171

had refused to allow any more prisoners to be brought in, as there was not the food or accommodation for them; after being take on to Sachzenhausen, and in February 1945 to Mauthausen, where Archambaud and John Young had earlier been murdered, he slipped out in a party which the Swiss Red Cross had permission to extract. He was seen there by the Channel Islander, Anthony Faramus.[78]

On August 10, Vogt was told by Kieffer privately that their department was withdrawing from Paris to Nancy.[79] The rest of the staff must have been notified soon afterwards, for the next few days were spent in going through their vast accumulation of papers, which they sorted into three lots, to take with them in their retreat, to destroy (a time-taking process) and simply to abandon:

> I am absolutely sure we left no mines or explosives at Avenue Foch, or important papers. We left Paris on August 17, in the evening. I do not know who came into the Avenue Foch after we left it, but I suppose the Resistance movements must have taken possession. We left Paris in perfect order and without haste; there was moreover no danger and Kieffer told me the Wehrmacht (army) would probably take possession of the building.[80]

The remark about mines was made in reply to a letter of mine telling him of a strange story I had heard from Madame

---

[78] Faramus telephoned me on July 18, 1954, after seeing the first advance extract from *The Starr Affair* in *The Sunday Empire News*, and came to see me later in the same day He gave me an account of Mauthausen, and of Starr at Mauthausen, which confirmed Starr's, note that this was before the book had appeared, so he could not have known what details were in my book

[79] Vogt, letter to author, December 3, 1950

[80] Vogt, letter to author, February 28, 1956

Aigrain. Her friend, Andrès, who had been arrested with her but got away (I cannot remember whether he had escaped or been released), had been the first person of Allied nationality to enter 84 Avenue Foch after its vacation by the Gestapo and SD; that he went in on his own, unofficially, from curiosity to see what papers were left and was blown up by a mine — or that was the accepted story but somebody else who had been into the premises soon afterwards told her the blood found was not in the same place as the body found, which must have been moved, and that the details (which she hesitated to give me exactly) were not consistent with his having been blown up by a mine but suggested murder; she had tried to probe this but had been warned off with the words, 'One is dead because he knew too much, there is no reason why there should be two' — for which reason she had left it alone.

On August 20, the Allies entered Paris.

Mysteriously, this was not quite the end of the radio-game. According to what Vogt told me:[81]

> When we withdrew from Paris in August 1944 we took with us a radio-line which we played fruitfully to London from Nancy, then from Offenburg, from Freiburg i. Brg, and from the side of Lake Constance right until April, 1945. At the end of January 1945 English or American agents were still being parachuted into our hands through our radio-link with London. These agents were at our request dropped near to Lake Constance. But I do not think they were agents of the French Section, I think they belonged to an American espionage service in London. We still had in Germany at the end of 1944 and in the beginning of 1945 two radio links with London, but in so far as I can tell neither of these circuits belonged to the French Section.

---

[81] Vogt, letter to author, September 12, 1954

Vogt calls it an espionage service because of something odd. The three agents parachuted spoke perfect German, and declared themselves to be SS Sturmbannführers. Kieffer was SS. Sturmbannführer. To support their claim, they produced what they said were SS Sturmbannführer identity cards. Kieffer, to discountenance them, laid his own on the table, so that they could see that theirs were different. No whit put out, they retorted blandly, 'Yours is out of date. All SD identity-cards are renewable three-monthly, now.'

Kieffer thought this was probably insolent bluff, yet he sent Vogt to Berlin to obtain an interview on his behalf with Kopkow, to find out the truth of it. It was the only time Vogt ever saw Kieffer's chief, and he felt mildly embarrassed at having to tell this important man of something that must sound rather silly. 'These prisoners we have taken tell us our papers are out of order...'

Kopkow's face took on a very curious expression. 'It had been intended to call in the existing ones and to issue new ones in this form,' he said, looking at the fakes. 'But none in this form have been issued yet.'

Plainly, he left Kopkow wondering who, in the very small number of persons who could have known of the intended change, could have betrayed it to the Allies.

But who were these men parachuted into Germany? General Gubbins's lecture to the United Services Club says nothing about a German Section. What service did they belong to? It must, in some sense, have been a successor to SOE or Kieffer's service would not have been handling its radio-circuits as though they had been the continuation of SOE's. But Kieffer's department had blown its cover when it 'signed' its last message to the French Section 'Gestapo'. Buckmaster's reply had shown that he understood. Whoever the 'successors' were, why had they not been made wise by SOE's experience?

XIII: TRIALS AND JUDGMENTS

The Unconditional Surrender left the Germans who had served in the SD and similar services fearful that they could be shot without trial, as having no rights. Probably that is why Kieffer submitted to Harold Cole's proposition that Cole should, posing as a behind the lines Intelligence agent, Captain Mason, present Kieffer to an American army HQ as a German who had helped him.

Vogt got rid of his uniform and presented himself at a farm, asking if he could help with the cows. As a boy he had sometimes milked the cows on his father's farm; after so long, he did not know if cows would give him their milk, but they did. He had been promoted to work in the dairy and was making cheeses when Americans found him. That was a year after the surrender, on May 29, 1946. The Americans put him in Dachau. After eleven months they gave him a clearance and passed him to the British, at Staumühler, on April 1, 1947. They hardly questioned him, but a Sergeant came from London asking him for a deposition about Starr, seeming to expect an adverse one. Vogt told him Starr had never given anyone or anything away, and wrote out a statement to that effect.

In mid-July, he was sent back to the Americans, who having cleared him once asked him if he knew for what purpose he had been returned to them. Not wanting him, they handed him over to the new German government, which put him back in Dachau, which had now reverted to German control. This authority gave him a De-Nazification Certificate and sent him to the British, who having cleared him once did not want him back again.

When he asked if, in that case, he might go to his home, they said, 'No,' because it was in the French zone; they allowed him to live in one of the cells, with the door open, so that he could walk in the town, returning for sleep and for meals. This continued until they wanted to close the camp, when they gave him permission to leave the British zone. As soon as he had arrived at his home a French Colonel called, very polite; there was no charge against him, he could be useful to them... Vogt had no intention of reentering Intelligence and refused.

In the end, as his wife was in French hands, he consented to go to Paris as a 'voluntary prisoner' to give help limited to the elucidation of certain matters of which he might have knowledge from his service at Avenue Foch. What they really wanted to know from him was which Allied agents turned traitor and who betrayed who. He felt himself faced with a moral problem. 'I did not want to be twice somebody's enemy, first to make him talk and then to tell he did it.'

He also felt he must not give false clearances, as to do that would devalue his genuine ones; so he evolved a way of putting things, which for some was not a total clearance yet would not cause them trouble. He denounced only when he saw that an innocent person was suspect for want of the culprit's being known. In the case of Déricourt, whom he knew only as Gilbert, he stated what he knew mainly for the memories of Prosper and Archambaud, of whose deaths he was shocked to learn. The violation of the pact he felt as the most shaming thing of any of which he had personal knowledge. The French told him they had asked the British for him in mid-July, 1947 and showed him the reply they had received saying they did not know where he was, dated just after his return by them to the Americans. The French were very cross about this, as at that time he could have given evidence in the trial of Déricourt; now Déricourt had been acquitted.

They were also very cross because Kieffer had been hanged by the British without being made available to them for questioning. Vogt was distressed to learn Kieffer had been hanged. 'I should have liked to have testified for him,' he told me. He had not known he was being tried.

John Starr, returned to England from Mauthausen Extermination Camp, had been called to the Judge Advocate General's Office, where he had been told that Kieffer was being tried and was asking for him as a witness. This was in March, 1947. Starr went immediately to Wuppertal, where the trial had already begun. He found himself the only witness for the defence. He said that to the best of his knowledge no member of the French Section had been tortured at Avenue Foch. The President of the Court asked him whether he could say he had seen all the prisoners; to this he had to answer, 'No'. He spoke of Kieffer's bringing round chocolate, biscuits and (though a non-smoker) cigarettes to the prisoners on Sunday mornings.

Actually, it was not the treatment of prisoners at Avenue Foch that was in question. Six uniformed commandos captured in Normandy had been shot. The order had come to Kieffer from his chief in Berlin and he had passed it on to those who had carried out the execution; it was with this that he was charged. He was sentenced to death. Starr saw Kieffer's face as he was sentenced, and was sure the look on it was one of amazement. As he left the court he made a bow to Starr. It was as if he had said, 'You did what you could.' In the mess afterwards, one of the officers of the court told Starr the

Prosecutor had expressed the very greatest astonishment at the sentence. It was carried out very quickly.

Vogt was discharged by the French with a *Non Lieu* in March, 1950, and set on a train for Germany. After spending the last eleven months in solitary confinement he was at first dazed by the people and traffic in the streets, but by June he had found employment in a bank. He received a paper issued jointly by the British, French, American and German De-Nazification authorities saying he was not wanted as a war criminal.

To the best of his knowledge, the only member of Kieffer's staff charged with ill-treatment of a prisoner was Rühl, who had beaten someone up, not at Avenue Foch but somewhere in the provinces. His advocate said he had been punished already in that when taken as a prisoner to England he had himself been beaten up. The French court sentenced him to two and a half years, and, the time he had spent in Allied hands already being taken into account, he was released immediately.[82]

Goetz and Placke had already been released, before Vogt. (Inspector Coupaye and Mangin of the DST when I met them with Starr on April 18, 1950, told me the Avenue Foch men who had been in London were at first very silent when they arrived; but after they began to gain confidence one of them said that when they were leaving London they were told, 'We have to hand you over to the French now, but it would be better not to tell them too much.') Placke, however, they believed to be now under the special protection of the British.

To turn to the Abwehr, Sergeant Bleicher was arrested in Holland and taken to London, where he was interrogated by Vera Atkins, and later in the year handed over to the French. In the rue des Saussaies he was received by Wybot and given a

---

[82] Letter from Vogt to author, March 31, 1951

room in which to write out his recollections at leisure. Why Bleicher needed to do it so fully is a mystery. He incriminated his former agents beyond necessity. Naturally, the French, who were preparing cases against Raoul Kiffer (Kiki), Roger Bardet and others wanted his evidence, but as one turns the pages of the long statement he made for the DST, one sees that he made no effort whatever to put things in a light that would help them. On the contrary, he made the most of the willingness, even the eagerness, they had displayed to betray their Resistance colleagues to him. Surely he must have realised that what he was writing out made the passing of death sentences inevitable. Did he want to destroy those who had worked for him, or was he simply putting himself in the good books of Wybot by giving him the utmost plenitude of the sort of information he wanted, regardless how he destroyed his former human tools? It is not surprising he came to be regarded as Wybot's tool.

Christmann was in Germany when the war ended. When he heard of the Unconditional Surrender he tore up his Abwehr and identity papers and disposed of them down the lavatory. Convinced the Allies would have him shot or hanged for the role he had played, and would search Germany for him, he went to the nearest British Military HQ and said, 'I am Richard Jolly, a French citizen escaped from concentration camp and I want to return to France.' The British CO could not give anyone a pass without papers. Christmann came back to him day after day, assuming a mien more and more distraught. 'I am Richard Jolly, a French citizen and I want to go to France.' Finally, the British CO gave him a paper saying, 'Permit bearer to leave the British Zone.' Once across the frontier, he made his way to Paris, where he unearthed a cache of gold bricks, gems and jewellery he had earlier deposited against a rainy day, and went down to the Riviera.

By selling the pieces one by one he was able to subsist for some time. One of the jewels was a sapphire he had bought from a Jew in Amsterdam. For the size of the stone, the price he had had to pay for it was modest; he supposed that was because the Jew had not dared to bargain with a German. He took the sapphire into a jeweller's in Nice and asked how much it was worth.

The jeweller said, 'Nothing, Monsieur; it's a fake.' As he was leaving the jeweller's two unpleasant types closed in upon him and told him they had seen him with the Abwehr and would denounce him unless he made it worth their while.

Christmann said, 'I have no money on me but I have something else,' and he gave them the sapphire. Later a big win at Monte Carlo enabled him to buy a draper's with a contraband nylons connection with Italy.

It was when he wanted to buy a car that he became too bold. To buy a car it was necessary to have an identity card. So he went into a police station and explained, 'I am Richard Jolly, a French citizen, born in Bordeaux. Returned from Concentration Camp, I have to obtain a new identity card, but I find my birth certificate was one of those destroyed when a bomb fell on the Registry of Births at Bordeaux. What shall I do?' The police told him he had to find two persons who could swear they had known him for before the war, for preference as a child in his parents' home, and that they had always known him as Richard Jolly, born in Bordeaux. He found two persons who, for a price, obliged.

But perhaps someone in the police station thought of the exploitation to which the destruction of the Bordeaux records made France vulnerable; at any rate someone in that police station looked at the circulated photographs of wanted men and recognised their visitor. A party was sent to apprehend him. 'Hands up!' he was told. They charged him in his assumed identity of Richard Jolly, a French citizen, with intelligence with the enemy. Seeing himself shot for intelligence with his own country, he cried, 'I am Richard Christmann, a German citizen. I am Richard Christmann of the Abwehr.'

It was almost exactly a year since the Unconditional Surrender. And now he was faced with having to prove that all his beautifully forged papers were forged.[83] He told me that he was beaten up (which is believable) and that he was put under 'sunlights'. Catching a glimpse of Bleicher, comfortably installed in a room of his own at the rue des Saussaies, 'writing out his memoirs' he was filled with fury. *'Bleicher ist ein Schwein!'* he said to me with venom — 'Every poor type who did him the smallest service he denounced.'

Christmann was in the end given the usual *Non Lieu* and set on a train that would not stop until it had crossed the German frontier. He was forbidden ever to re-enter France or to enter any French territory overseas.

When last I saw him he had an office full of baby-foods and Complan. He showed me a letter from Glaxo Ltd., Greenford, appointing him their sole representative in an African country.

Colonel Giskes naturally received a clearance. The murder of the greater number of the North Pole prisoners was not his fault; indeed, he had obtained a promise from Berlin they would be spared. Their subsequent murder parallels that of 'Prosper', 'Archambaud' and the other members of the French

---

[83] I take this account from a book-length unpublished typescript memoir, in German, of his year of freedom, *The Tear of Richard Jolly*, by Christmann, which Christmann lent me

Section whose lives had been guaranteed under the pact. There is no reason to doubt Kieffer's good faith.

To come to Allied nationals involved with the Germans, the Cat was handed over by the British to the French for trial, and sentenced to death; the sentence was commuted to one of imprisonment in perpetuity, of which she served twelve years.

Perhaps the strangest turn was given to the Cat's story when I went to Hamburg in the summer of 1955 to see Colonel Giskes. Casually, we mentioned the Cat.

'I knew of her in Paris before I was posted to Holland,' he said.

I hardly believed I had heard right, but he was firm. One of his men, he said, had happened to be in a café and had heard the woman at the next table and a man talking. 'He was not even on duty, but he was alone and he could not help hearing that they were talking of spying.' After that, a watch was kept on her and her associates.

'But when was this?'

'I can only say it was before the summer of 1941, when I was posted to Holland.'

I protested that Borchers in his book *La Chatte* gave such a vivid account of how the group was traced to its heart through the uncovering of one of its outposts in Cherbourg... 'Could your people have lost them, after the first report, so that they needed to be traced again...?'

'I left the case to my successor, that is all I can say,' said Colonel Giskes thoughtfully. He had not made an immediate series of arrests because he thought it more interesting to let the situation develop under observation; perhaps his successor did the same, and the *coup* was from below, by sub or junior officers not in the know.

But, I said, it was not a single *coup* made on one night. Between the first arrest in Cherbourg and the arrest of the Cat a lot of days elapsed, during which Borchers certainly communicated with those above him.

Perhaps it was too late to stop the ball once it had started rolling, said Giskes. Once it started it had to go on, even if it interfered with what had been the higher plan...

After a pause, he asked, 'The men who made this coup, were they rewarded by promotion?'

Bleicher, I recalled, had never been promoted above Sergeant, which had always puzzled me. 'And Captain Borchers?' asked Giskes. Then something at the end of Borchers' book came back to me. 'He was relieved of his post, sent home to Germany, without thanks and without explanation. But he thought it was because he had one night drunk too much...'

Colonel Giskes looked at me with the strangest expression.

The affair of René Hardy made headlines in the French press for so long that, again, I do not want to do more than recapitulate it here. Briefly, at his original trial he was acquitted, by the Cour de la Seine on January 24, 1947. Only after his acquittal was it discovered that his journey from Marseilles to Paris on June 7 or 8 had been broken by an arrest, and that he had been in Barbie's hands prior to the mass arrests. In principle, French law is the same as ours: a man cannot be tried twice on the same charge; but in certain very exceptional cases he can, where at the first trial a fact of immense magnitude has been totally suppressed, so that it can be said that in a sense the court that sat was not trying the correct issue at all. There is then the necessary *fait nouveau* to reopen the case upon the right grounds.

At Hardy's second trial, which opened two months later, at the Tribunal Militaire, the one that counts, he was defended by Maître Maurice Garçon, one of the greatest French advocates, whose handling of this case has been considered his masterpiece. He started by saying he would not build upon the former judgement, but recognised the immense wave of public feeling which had followed upon the discovery of the mis-statement upon which the accused had based the defence which gained him an acquittal. He then went on to put it to the court that the lie itself did not prove his client was guilty; he now explained that he had concealed his arrest from his colleagues because, when he learned of the arrest of General Delestraint, he thought that if they knew of his arrest they would suppose him to have betrayed General Delestraint, which genuinely was not the case. His silence in the first place obviously made it impossible for him to own up when arrests of even greater magnitude took place. Obviously, it would be thought he had betrayed Jean Moulin and the whole CNR. That did not prove that he had betrayed them. Hardy was acquitted for the second time.

It must be said that a deposition obtained from Barbie, inculpating Hardy in such exaggerated terms as to suggest malignancy, probably did him more good than harm, for who would want to condemn a Frenchman on the word of a Gestapo chief of particularly bad repute? Nevertheless, I do not quite see why some French people think the Americans put Barbie up to it. He was in American hands and they would not allow him to come to court to testify, which was why a deposition had to be taken, but even if they were protecting him because they had a use for him, there really seems no reason why they should wish to pervert justice in the Hardy affair.

Nevertheless, there is some mystery behind the Americans and Barbie, though I do not know what it is. Why did they protect him? It was under his aegis that Jean Moulin was so hideously tortured that he died within days. Even Boemelburg is reported to have been disgusted. It does seem unfair that Kieffer, who had a certain amount of decency, should have been hanged, while Barbie survived to write articles from Brazil.

The oddest offshoot from the Hardy affair was, however, the intervention of a woman known as Mona la Blonde; correctly, Marie-Delphine Reimeringer. Alsatian, born at Metz while it was still German, she had like all such persons a problem of nationality. German by blood and birth, she became French with the cession to France in 1918; but not in the spirit. During the German occupation of France in the Second World War she worked in the office of the Gestapo at Blois under Ludwig Bauer. After the liberation, she found herself charged with treason and sentenced to twenty years. On April 29, 1947, *Samedi-Soir* carried a headline: '*Mona la Blonde affirme "Hardy est innocent."*' She had, apparently, written a letter from her cell to Hardy's *Juge d'Instruction* claiming that not Hardy but Culioli gave away the meeting of the chiefs of the CNR at Caluire, and Prosper and his network as well. She made a great number of errors. For instance, she placed the arrest of Culioli on June 15, whereas it was on June 21, the same day as the *coup* at Caluire. The chief reason why this part of her allegation fell at once was, however, that the total separation of RF and of the French Section made it quite impossible Culioli should know anything of the organisation of the CNR or the projected meeting of its chiefs at Caluire. If the purpose of Madame Reimeringer's intervention was to clear Hardy, it was vain, for her accusation against Culioli was not entertained in this connection; but she did get him charged with Intelligence with the Enemy on the basis of her allegation that it was he who betrayed Prosper.

In this she had a supporter in Maurice Lequeux, whom she had known in prison at Blois, and who was serving a sentence of which the original term was ten years' hard labour.

Culioli was charged in August 1947, and after the usual lengthy *instruction* tried on June 9, 1948. Madame Reimeringer alleged that it was Culioli who had led the Gestapo to the Hotel Mazagran, where Prosper was arrested. When it was pointed out that Culioli had been too heavily wounded to have walked at that time, she said he had directed the party whilst being carried on Bauer's back. This would have constituted a spectacle and nobody had seen any such spectacle.

Lequeux of course witnessed for the prosecution, and so did Flower (Gaspar), who distracted the court with the story of how he had obtained from London a pill to poison Culioli but been dissuaded by Archambaud.

Culioli repudiated the accusation that he had betrayed Prosper, but explained the pact, as Archambaud had explained it to him, and declared having given away the four arms dumps on the premises of Couffrant, Gatignon, Le Meur and Cordelet and written notes to the four householders saying he was sorry to be obliged to give them away.

During the *instruction*, a paper had been delivered to the *Juge d'Instruction* signed by thirty-three members of Culioli's network, expressing confidence in his integrity and willingness to testify for him at his trial. Amongst the signatories were Couffrant, Gatignon and the widow of Cordelet, the only one to have died in captivity.

The court returned a mixed verdict; it found Culioli not guilty of intelligence with the enemy (i.e. not guilty of the betrayal of Prosper), but guilty of acts prejudicial to the national defence. Because of the mitigating circumstances no sentence was imposed and he was immediately released.

In defiance of his advocate's advice to let well alone, he asked for a re-trial.

A remarkable letter written by one of the other women employees of the Gestapo at Blois, Geneviève Danelle, under sentence of death, though written before the first trial arrived at the Tribunal Militaire only after the trial was over:

Monsieur le President,

I learn that the trial of Mr Culioli is to begin soon. I worked in the German service at Blois directed by Mr Bauer and seconded by Mme. Reimeringer... and often heard speak of Culioli... The members of our department were impressed by the attitude of Culioli, who kept his head in a remarkable way. I wish to make the point that Mme. Reimeringer deplored to Bauer that she had not been able to obtain all the information she wanted and recommended the employment of brutality, to which Bauer replied, 'With idealists that does not work; and Culioli is an idealist.'

I do not know what Mr Culioli is accused of before your court-martial, but everything said of him at Blois was in his favour, as being a man of great courage, which incites me to make this declaration.

I heard some months ago that the depositions of Mme. Reimeringer had not been in his favour, but quite to the contrary.

I am with just reason astonished by the contradiction existing between what I heard concerning Culioli and what Mona seems to have declared. For everything I know is to his honour. I would point out that I write these lines without knowing the result of my appeal for mercy. Whether I am to be reprieved or executed, I maintain the present declaration.

Geneviève Danelle

The second trial of Culioli was on March 17, 1949, before the Tribunal Militaire at Metz. Mona Reimeringer, who had obtained a remission of her twenty years' sentence and was freed, was again the chief accuser. Geneviève Danelle had been executed; but her letter was read out.

Maurice Lequeux accused again, maintaining the network in the north of Touraine of which he had been found guilty of betraying, had been betrayed by Culioli; indeed in *La Bataille* of September 17, 1947, he had declared, 'If one admits that Culioli did not talk, then it must have been me.' The outcome of the re-trial was therefore grave for him. He exhibited a letter written him by Colonel Buckmaster:

20 August, 1947

Dear Monsieur,

    Returned yesterday from a business trip, I have just received your letter of August 16. I am very happy to learn the result of the trial of which you have been the innocent victim ...

The President of the Court, puzzled, asked, 'Does he mean the trial which ended in your being sentenced to hard labour?'

'Yes, Monsieur le President.'

'The English have really a sense of humour,' said the President.[84]

The Abbé Guillaume found this letter of Colonel Buckmaster so incredible that he sent me a photocopy of it (I suppose made from the photocopy supplied by the Tribunal Militaire to Culioli's lawyer) to ask me whether the hand in which it was written was indeed Buckmaster's. I said I thought it was; and certainly the address at the top was Buckmaster's.

At this second trial, Culioli obtained a simple acquittal.

---

[84] Guillaume, *La Sologne*

The strangest case, however, was that of Déricourt. He relinquished his commission in the RAF Volunteer Reserve on August 19, 1944, immediately enlisted in the Free French Air Force and was shot down over Châteauroux on September 9, with multiple injuries, necessitating long hospitalisation. On recovery, he became a pilot for Air France, flying between Paris and London; this employment he lost when, on April 11, 1946, he was apprehended at Croydon attempting to smuggle bullion. In the meantime, the DST had been studying German testimonies; on November 26, 1946, Déricourt was charged with Intelligence with the Enemy.

In his deposition for the DST of that month, Déricourt avowed dealings with Placke, Goetz and Boemelburg, but said it was two German pilots he had known before the war who called on him, and who put him in touch with the SD before he was aware of what was happening, and he found himself a prisoner at liberty. He declared having given the Germans details of two operations, one at Soucelles and one possibly at Pocé-sur-Cisse. His account of the operation at Soucelles and of the surveillance in the train by the group of unwholesome looking men first seen on the platform at Le Mans tallies with Marc's, given independently and at liberty.

Déricourt said, probably truthfully, that he did not know whether or not any arrests had been made as the result of his having given Goetz details of these operations, as he had no way to check up upon what damage, if any, occurred in his wake. He had understood from the Germans that they would make no arrests in consequence of his information, but allowed it was possible he had been bluffed. On his recall to London in February 1944 he had not disclosed his dealings with the Germans, partly because he could not bring himself to admit truth in any charges made by Frager, but above all because he was afraid that the English would respond to confidence by putting him in gaol, and, as the news of that was bound to leak back to the Germans through Frager, Bardet and Bleicher, Boemelburg, abandoning hope that he would return to perform former services, would at once order the arrest-of all the members of his team, whom he had been obliged to leave in France. The members of his team were not his accomplices.

One must remember that the French authorities had no way of checking whether or not any of the agents landed by Déricourt's aircraft had been arrested, since they did not know how many there had been or who they were. When Culioli was charged, Prosper was wrongly described upon the charge-sheet as 'by his right name, Lord Cole'. The Abbé Guillaume told me his guess was that Lord was a corruption of Harold, containing four of the same letters; there had been some difference of testimony at that date as to whether Cole was Prosper or (according to Madame Reimeringer) Archambaud, but no one had grasped at that date that Harold Cole was a separately existing individual. How anybody had come to confuse the traitor of the MI9 escape routes with any member of the *Prosper* team is a mystery, and it may be that something lies behind this. I toy with the idea that Cole, during some of the time he was imagined to be in prison, actually impersonated one or the other, spreading wider the misfortunes of the *Prosper* network. But I mention the confusion here simply to show the disadvantage under which the French were labouring while bringing these trials, in that they were trying offences committed or alleged to have been committed against the British networks, without the knowledge only the British possessed.

The eighteen months' *instruction* Déricourt spent in Fresnes, where he was a fellow prisoner of Culioli, Bardet, Kiffer and Claude Jouffret.

It was Bodington who saved Déricourt. On the morning of June 8, 1948, the defence witnesses collected by Marc were heard (or in some cases sent written statements), persons who had been passengers into or out of France aboard his aircraft in safety, General Zeller, General Elie, Madame Felix Gouin, Madame Pierre Bloch, François Mitterand, Roualt, Victor Gerson, Fille-Lambie, Rachet, Didier-Daurant, Wuyard...

But it was in the afternoon the tide turned, when Bodington went into the box. It was not Marc who found Bodington. Unless Déricourt's wife saw him he seems to have come forward of his own accord. Déricourt, he said, had told him of his relations with the Germans and he had advised him to maintain them. It was the natural thing. If he had to start all over again, he would start with Déricourt.

The panel of military judges, after the briefest retirement, returned a verdict of Not Guilty.

Nevertheless, what had happened left the French profoundly troubled. What nobody doubted was that Bodington had come officially.

After the publication of my first study of this affair, *Double Webs* (Putnam, 1958), my friend Dame Irene Ward[85] sent a copy to Harold Macmillan, then Prime Minister, asking about this, and he made an appointment for her to be received at the Foreign Office by Lord Lansdowne. Lord Lansdowne told Dame Irene it was not the Foreign Office which had authorised Déricourt to enter into relations with the Germans and he rather thought he must have done it on his own responsibility. Neither was it the Foreign Office which had

---

[85] Today Baroness Ward

sent Bodington to give evidence at his trial. Major Bodington, since he resigned his commission after the war, had become a private citizen. He had not sought the advice of the Foreign Office on this matter, and what he had done was on his own responsibility.

After Déricourt's trial came the trial, together, of Roger Bardet, Raoul Kiffer (Kiki) and Claude Jouffret. On December 9, 1949, Bardet and Kiffer were sentenced to death and Jouffret to four years. The sentences on Bardet and Kiffer were later commuted and both were released after serving only a few years. Jouffret was released immediately, and was given shelter by Déricourt and his wife.

Déricourt kept in touch with me until shortly before his plane crashed in Laos on November 20, 1962.1 have entered into his story in full in *The Chequered Spy* (George Mann, 1975), which is entirely about him.

Bodington died in Plymouth on July 3, 1974.[86]

---

[86] The Foreign Office; letter from Colonel Boxshall to author, dated July 8, 1974.

XIV: REFLECTIONS

The unsolved mystery remains that of the radio-game. The prisoners thought there must be treachery in London or that London was making sacrifices to some secret end. In Holland after the war a Dutch Parliamentary Commission sat for more than two years on North Pole, questioning all available Germans as well as Dutchmen. To its Chairman, Dr Donkers, the Foreign Office sent a statement[87] assuring him that the British authorities responsible had had no end other than that declared to the Netherlands authorities and that the penetration was due solely to the operation of German counter-intelligence, which as it took place at an early stage 'led to a complete German control'.

An important contributory cause of its continuance was that the absence of security checks was ignored. It explained the separation of SOE and the Intelligence Service and that the bulk of the records of the former had been destroyed, which placed serious obstacles in the way of an enquiry; but it stated that when the Intelligence Service learned that SOE operations had been penetrated it immediately notified SOE; this was not until May, 1943. It exonerated Colonel de Bruyne, in that he was not in the position to check the texts of signals, and Major Bingham, who was not in charge at the time the original penetration occurred, and as soon as he took charge (in March, 1943) insisted on agents' being parachuted not to reception committees but blind. By these two eliminations, the

---

[87] The whole of the Foreign Office statement to Dr Donkers is reproduced in *Inside North Pole*, Pieter Dourlein (Kimber, 1953), pp 175-80

responsibility was left upon the first British officer in charge of the section, who was not named but was Major Blunt. He has never come before the public (somebody told me he went to Australia, which may or may not be true) so that one is without any insight into what happened such as might be afforded by personality.

On May 3, 1974, *The Times* ran on the front page a sensational article under the headline '*Rivalry in London led to deaths of agents*'. It announced that Dr Lou de Jong head of the Institute of War Documentation in Amsterdam, had stated in the Dutch official history, *The Kingdom of the Netherlands in the Second World War*, that MI6 (the Intelligence Service), when it realised the German control, failed to warn SOE. As this seemed in contradiction to paragraph 15 of the Foreign Office statement to Dr Donkers, I wrote both to the Dutch Embassy, asking if the work had been translated into English, and, on being informed there was no translation, to the appropriate correspondent of *The Times*, asking whether what Dr de Jong said in his book in effect contradicted our Foreign Office. As I received no reply, I wrote care of the Dutch Embassy, to Dr de Jong, saying I did not read Dutch and asking him if he would be kind enough to tell me in English what he had said about this in his book. From his reply, it was plain he had said in his book nothing we had not known for years from Colonel Giskes on the one hand and the Foreign Office statement to Dr Donkers on the other. He claimed he had not alleged that the Intelligence Service had failed to inform SOE. If this is so, the passage in *The Times* must have arisen from a misunderstanding of what he had written.

Major Blunt has not thrust himself on the public, but Colonel Buckmaster has not shunned it. His books,[88] however,

---

[88] *Specially Employed*, Maurice Buckmaster (Batchworth Press, 1952)

have been adventure stories with nothing about agents being dropped into German hands as the result of the radio-game. Perhaps this would never have come out if I had not revealed it in *The Starr Affair*. In the polemic which followed its publication, he declared that only one of the circuits became German controlled. Even this admission surprised Colonel Spooner, who told me that neither during the war nor since had he heard that *any* became German controlled. He had been given to understand that the 'sending' of an operator was impossible to imitate. He showed me a book, *The Secret Corps*, by Ferdinand Tuhoy (Murray, 1920), inviting me to read a paragraph on p. 153, referring to an invention by which the sending oscillations of a radio operator could be photographed, and used to check the identity of sender. He was only surprised, seeing that this thing had been invented by 1920, that it had taken SOE until mid-1943 to get down to using it. Spooner had been head of the Security Training School at Beaulieu; he was not a radio-man; he had to take it from Brigadier Nicholls that the thing worked. I suggested to him that perhaps the unaffected sendings of operators could be distinguished by this invention, like unaffected handwritings, but that sendings, like handwritings, could be so successfully imitated as to deceive. He replied, that he had been told the thing was watertight.

'So what do you think?' I asked him.

'I don't know,' he said, troubled.

---

and *They Fought Alone*, Maurice Buckmaster (Odhams, 1958). The latter contains on p 75 a map of France on which Organisers' areas are marked off. A large area in the north-east is marked 'Pickersgill' Pickersgill never for a moment organised that area. He and Macalister were arrested before they even reached Paris and replaced by Placke and Holdorf who organised it under German control from the beginning.

In 1955 my friend Dame Irene Ward spoke with Brigadier Nicholls, and he gave her the two sets of photographed oscillations. The difference between the two sets of sendings was certainly very plain, even to our untrained eyes, and he had, she told me, been absolutely categoric that no substitution could go undetected. He would not listen to anything else. 'North Pole had not registered with him.' His radio responsibilities had been world-wide, and she doubted whether he had heard of it.

Nine years later, Professor Foot was to admit the radio-game in the official history, in the cases of all the circuits I had mentioned in *The Starr Affair* and more besides. He also found a record by Bourne-Paterson, who succeeded Bodington as Buckmaster's second-in-command, that 'the Gestapo were encouraged to believe that we were unaware of the extent of their penetration, and deliveries of stores were continued to circuits known to be German controlled, in order to give time for new circuits to establish themselves.' Professor Foot comments:[89]

> At first glance it will seem odd that tons of expensive arms and explosives should be delivered, in still more expensive aircraft, by almost irreplaceable aircrews, straight into German hands....

Yes, it did seem odd, to agents in the field or prisoner at Avenue Foch, who had not Professor Foot to explain to them that when cargoes of materials were parachuted straight into German hands it was sometimes on purpose, but that when this was done with human beings it was always by mistake.

Colonel Buckmaster has stated:[90]

---

[89] Official History, p 328

[90] *Statement by Colonel Maurice Buckmaster, OBE,* appended to *Inside*

Perhaps the most appalling accusation made against us is that we *deliberately* sent out agents into the hands of the Germans … I flatly deny these monstrous and intolerable accusations...

I do not wish to gun for a man who is, today, so I understand, doing valuable work inspiring young people. Spooner's portrayal of him to me was of a man industrious but in some ways immature. 'Buckmaster is a boy-scout. His heroes could have stepped almost out of the *Boys' Own Mag*, clean-shaven public schoolboys who died keeping a stiff upper lip, or else rough diamonds.'

This brings me to a moral criticism of SOE which I make with some hesitation as it may give offence because it is absolutely radical. The work of SOE was sabotage; not merely soft sabotage, such as the manufacture of non-striking matches or non-exploding shells, such as might be achieved by the workers, but acts violent in themselves, bound to invite violent reprisals upon the civilian population. The organisation has been much idealised and there is no doubt of the idealism with which many went into it, but my first glimpse of what it really did came when I talked with Vogt. We were speaking of the Garrys. He said they were a nice couple, newly married and so genuinely concerned about one another that, as a human being, he felt in a way sorry to have to spoil their happiness by arresting them and seeing them into separate cells, in prison; but Garry had derailed a train, carrying German soldiers. That was not a matter which could be lightly viewed, as much life had been lost, and such a man, left at liberty, might do the same again.

Garry told him his wife knew nothing of his Resistance activities. Vogt told me he affected to believe this, as his

---

SOE, E H Cookridge (Barker, 1966), p 603

228

impression was that Garry was the dominant partner and that his wife simply went along with what he did; he did not really think she was ignorant (and indeed she assured me she was not ignorant) that he was in Resistance up to the hilt; nevertheless he did not know whether she knew he derailed a train. He never asked her, never told her; but sometimes he wondered whether such a gentle person as she was could really have known, or if she knew approved, an action which caused so much loss of life. The soldiers were, from the Allied point of view, the enemy, but boxed in a train they were helpless, not 'killed in action' in the ordinary sense, and surely so to murder them was questionable, even according to the rules of war, which he did not profess to know.

I wondered then if Noor Inayat Khan (Madeleine), an equally gentle girl, a Sufi mystic's child, brought up in the devotional religious atmosphere and unbelievably idealistic, realised, when she was asked to hazard her life as a radio operator to the Resistance, what it was she was abetting. Resistance was a word conjuring up a heroic self-sacrifice to which one could be dedicated, for which one could offer one's life; but her first contact was Garry. Did she know about the train?

Cohen told me Denise derailed a train, but I do not think Vogt knew this.

And do most people realise, that derailment or blowing up of a train in most cases meant killing not only the German soldiers aboard it but the French engine-driver, the stoker, and the whole train crew; even if it was only a goods or munitions train, these were still aboard. Déricourt was amongst those who did not appreciate sacrifice of French railway crews. Weil, to his credit, refused to be party to railway sabotage in ways that must involve killing the French train crews.

Professor Foot shows in his book proudly a photograph of a derailed engine; he does not tell us what happened to the driver. This was the very sort of work SOE set out to do, and to question it is to question fundamentals.

Assassinations were commonplace. Colonel Giskes received over the North Pole circuits instructions from London to assassinate particular Dutch citizens who collaborated with the Germans. Yeo-Thomas designated a certain member of RF Section to me as 'our rat-killer'. Presumably the persons he was instructed to kill were in truth traitors to the Allies, but killings could only be done without trial. The very scrupulous might insist upon cornering and capturing an individual and giving him a chance to say something for himself first, but at best it was a kangaroo court; in other cases a killing was made without warning. When action is taken in this way, there is the possibility of 'executing' the innocent. Flower obtained from London a poison pill with which to kill Culioli, who has been found completely honourable. And where such violence is allowed, there lurks always the possibility that private murder from private motive may be dressed up as a Resistance killing. I am not saying that it happened; I know only that the suspicion it did happen has been voiced to me by many, I am not now speaking specially of SOE but of the whole of the Resistance, which it did so much to enflame.

Colonel Spooner made the comment that at Baker Street there seemed to him too 'Too much "Will you?" and not enough "You will".' He appreciated that his own preference for formal discipline seemed to some there blimpish; on the other hand, where instructions of gravity had to be given, it was a protection to those having to carry them out if they came in the form of orders, so that there should be clarity as to who was responsible.

Colonel George Starr, 'Hilaire', when he came to tea with me at my London flat, told me a disturbing story. Some time after the end of the war he received a desperate appeal from three men of his former network who found themselves imprisoned, charged with the murder of a certain local man. Colonel Starr remembered the instruction for this killing, which had come from London in the form of a radio-telegramme, but of course this had not been preserved. He got in touch with Buckmaster, but Buckmaster knew nothing about it. George Starr therefore flew to Bordeaux and went to the Police Station. There he took the whole thing on himself and, leaving London out of it, simply said that he had ordered this killing. 'As a matter of fact, they didn't look wildly pleased.' It came to him that the idea of an Englishman's taking upon himself to order the assassination of a French citizen was not one which appealed to them. However, they merely placed paper and a pen in front of him and asked him to put in writing what he had said. This he did, and the three men were released.

All this was the darker side of Churchill's historic injunction to 'set Europe ablaze.' Colonel Spooner had felt the gravity of it after the assassination of Heidrich.

Spooner himself had organised the assassination of Heidrich. Heidrich was an arch-persecutor of the Jews and an odious human being, and he had no compunction about training men to kill men. But because of the terrible revenge taken by the Germans against the people of Lidice, he wished he had not done it. That was something he would have to carry to his death. (His voice, always unclear because he spoke with his pipe in his mouth, died almost into inaudibility.) 'That did not come through Buckmaster. That came through another channel.' But he thought that SOE tended generally to be too regardless of the reprisals taken against the civilian population for the acts of sabotage it carried out, and that phrases like 'we must have him bumped off... rubbed out...' picked up from American films, were used without realisation of what they meant.

When I read Professor Foot's book, it seems to me monstrous that Spooner was not taken into confidence about the deception game with regard to the radios. He occupied a very responsible position. Surely he should not have been left to puzzle over it, years after the war, just like me. And to think that he had to learn about the radio-game from me — a civilian and an outsider who never heard of SOE until after the war and picked it up from Starr and Vogt!

Spooner thought it was a mistake of SOE 'to underestimate the enemy'. He had tried to prepare agents mentally for the sort of interrogation they might, if caught, have to undergo, but he had not reckoned on a Vogt. It had occurred to him that pressure might take the form not of straight brutality but of attempts to disconcert by the unexpected. 'The unexpected throws one off keel.' He had tried to prepare them for the unexpected — that was why, at the mock Gestapo interrogations to which trainees were subjected at Beaulieu they were often required to do merely odd things, like standing on a table. He had not expected the unexpected to take the form of afternoon-tea. He had not anticipated the extremely subtle moral problems that could be presented by someone as human as Vogt. Of course, it was known practice to have one nice interrogator... 'But Vogt is genuinely nice,' I said. 'Of course,' he replied. 'He couldn't do it convincingly otherwise. But it was clever of Kieffer to see the use that could be made of someone like that.'

An ex-regular officer of the Indian Army, externally curmudgeon, stiff in movements and without graces, his crusty carapace concealed a surprisingly nimble mind, realism, and an unusual capacity for looking at things straight, which commanded my respect. Spooner is dead now. I wish I could tell him his stature grows with the years.

One of the things Spooner deplored was the ever-increasing number of persons employed at the London end of SOE. It not only made security more difficult (Marjorie Spooner put in that on two occasions when she took a taxi to Baker Street the taxi-driver said, 'Spy Headquarters?'); as people got their friends into it, with an eye to business openings after the war, there came to be a lot of rather light people whose sense of responsibility for what was happening in the field was remote.

So one had this problem, that both at the London end and in France, there were too many people in the organisation. Déricourt declared it was the fault of giving military ranks to SOE men. 'In an army, promotion goes with the number of men commanded — between the ranks and the numbers commanded there is a link, all the way up — the highest has the most men,' and so everyone wanted to be able to report what a lot of people he had under him, in order to be promoted. In espionage it was vital not to have unnecessary people, and it was a mistake to have given officers' ranks. This seems to me valid, radical criticism. In London it had been explained to me by Selwyn Jepson that they were given officers' ranks in the hope that if they were able to state them on capture the Germans might abstain from having them shot as spies. (In parenthesis, I was fascinated by Len Deighton's remark in one of his novels that people involved in spying shrink from being called spies, preferring to call themselves agents; generally, I fancy that is true — but Déricourt always referred to himself as a spy.)

There is another reason why I have long felt that the officers' ranks engendered a false climate. The lives which they had to live in the field, in plain clothes, under false identities, were spy-like rather than soldier-like. They had to develop the way of thinking and the reflexes of spies, or they would have gone under in no time. Therefore, to require of them then a wholly soldierly standard — name, rank and number — was not fair. They were the victims of a double standard.

With spies, it seems to be understood that if they are cornered they work for the other side, avoiding doing more harm than they can help, and providing they take the earliest opportunity of returning to their own side, enriched — like bees with honey on their legs — with all the knowledge they have gathered whilst on the other side, they are forgiven. The mentality is quite different. SOE was an awkward hybrid in which they did not know where they were. (From this point of view, even the Cat may have been misjudged.)

The infinite subtlety of mind developed by a cornered man, for whom worlds of significance turned upon a hair, found no response in persons in London who were amateurs in clandestine work. In England we find it easier to credit our leaders with muddle than with Machiavellian cunning; on the continent it is the other way about. *Perfide Albion!* Yet even on the continent belief in a diabolic master-plan in London is weakening. Madame Balachowsky, when I first met her, averred the English were not imbeciles, 'They knew what they were doing!' Yet even her certainty about this weakened. In her long letter to me of December 20, 1958, she began by assuming London from mysterious motives put Madeleine into contact with Placke on purpose, but lower down she wrote:

I do not imagine London knowingly parachuted people to German reception. What would have been the use of it?

None, that I can see. I believe in a total incompetence of the service...

Since I wrote my earlier books, I have had glimpses of what happened at the London end, and what I believe is this: warnings were received but were discounted. The messages from Madeleine, Déricourt and Cohen saying Prosper, Archambaud and Denise had been arrested were all received, but were discounted. Archambaud's radio set was transmitting to them, so those who said he had been arrested must have been mistaken; probably they had not seen him for a few days and had therefore merely imagined him arrested. He did not give his double security-check, but it must be he was just careless ... I even talked with a most sincere and delightful English lady who said to me, 'But they *did* forget their security-checks sometimes; we had sometimes to remind them...' There was a kind of psychological inability to grasp that the worst had happened.

I do not want to attempt to evaluate the military contribution of SOE. I am aware that it had its successes. It just happened that I came upon things that were horrifying.

I do not want to talk about lessons for the future, because I hope there will not be a future in which people have to conduct operations of this sort. I do not call myself a pacifist, because pacifists tend to be such militant people; quite simply, when I see war I see a vast idiocy, and I hope we have no more of it. My remaining interest is in the people. I have the impression that two or three of those I came to know had emerged from the long night of German concentrations camp or Allied prison more deeply thinking than they went in. That is the meagre harvest.

DATES FOR REFERENCE

1941
October 17-24: Arrests Villa des Bois and vicinity
November 18: The Cat arrested
December 11 (?): Cole arrested, goes over

1942
February 26/27: The Cat fetched to England
March 6: Lauwers arrested; start of Operation North Pole
March: De Malval places Villa Isabelle at disposal of London
April 1: De Vomécourt parachuted back
April 24: Wolters arrested
April 25: De Vomécourt arrested
May, end of: Cartaud arrested, goes over
July: Jacqueline landed by felucca
September 24/25: 'Denise' and Lise de Baissac parachuted
October 1/2: 'Prosper' parachuted
October 20: Girard ('Carte') fetched to London
November 2: 'Archambaud' parachuted
November 2: Seven felucca passengers arrived at Villa Isabelle

1943
January 22/23: Déricourt and Worms parachuted
March: Marsac arrested, then Bardet, who goes over
April 15/16: Peter Churchill and Odette arrested
April 22/23: Déricourt fetched to London
April 22: Tambour sisters arrested
May 5: Déricourt parachuted back

May 13: 'Prosper' fetched to London

May 20: Square Clignancourt imbroglio

June 9: Capucines imbroglio

June 9: General Delestraint arrested

June 15/16: Two Canadians parachuted

June 20: 'Prosper' parachuted back

June 21: Chiefs of CNR arrested at Caluire

June 21: Culioli, 'Jacqueline' and two Canadians arrested

June 24: 'Prosper', 'Archambaud' and 'Denise' arrested

July 1: Worms and Guerne arrested

July 1: Grignon staff arrested

July 2: Balachowsky arrested

July 18: John Starr arrested

July22/23: Bodington and Agazarian parachuted back

August: Frager meets Bleicher

August 15/16: Bodington fetched to London

September 7: Rousset arrested

October 13: Madeleine arrested

October 18: Garry arrested

October 20/21: Frager fetched to London

November 15/16: Fatality at Soucelles

December 1: Escaped North Pole agents Dourlein and Ubbink, reach Spain

1944

February 7/8: Men parachuted to 'Madeleine' circuit

February 8/9: Déricourt obeys recall to London

February 29/March 1: Antelme, Lee and Madeleine Damerment parachuted to 'Madeleine' circuited. Men parachuted to Rousset circuit.

March 2/3: Men parachuted to Canadian circuit

March 7: Men parachuted to Rousset circuit

May: Starr engineers S. phone fiasco which ends radio-game
in France
June 6: D-Day
July 2 (?): Frager arrested
August 17: Avenue Foch staff withdraw from Paris

BIOGRAPHIES

Agazarian, Jack; 'Marcel'. 'Jacques Chevalier'; radio operator shared between 'Prosper' and Déricourt and others; parachuted end of July, 1942; arrested July, 1943 when keeping a rendezvous in Bodington's place, executed.

Antelme, Joseph France Antoine; 1st mission 'Reynaud', parachuted November, 1942, returned by one of Déricourt's aircraft March 17/18, 1943; 2nd mission 'Antoine', reinfiltrated, Organiser Bricklayer, returned by another of Déricourt's aircraft July 19/20, 1943; 3rd mission parachuted February 29/March 1 to German reception; executed at Gross Rosen, early September, 1944

'Antoine', see Antelme, also de Malval

'Anton', see Bodens

'Archambaud', see Norman

'Arnaud', see Rabinovitch, also Christmann

Balachowsky, Prof.; 'Serge', important sub-agent of the *Prosper* network, arrested July 1, 1943; deported to Buchenwald; survived probably because of Placke's intervention in getting him classified as a scientist; used this position to make possible the escape of Yeo-Thomas, Peulevé and Hessel

Bardet, Roger; started in *Carte* network, after schism became Frager's second in command; arrested following Marsac affair; then turned into agent of Bleicher, to whom he betrayed a number of people, including Frager; after the war condemned to death by the French, sentence commuted to one of imprisonment now out

Basin, Francis; 'Olive'; Organiser of network on Riviera coast, landed from HMS Fidelity September 19, 1941, Organiser

Urchin, Riviera, arrested August 14, 1942, escaped a year later; despatched to England on board one of Déricourt's aircraft August 19/20, 1943

Bégué, Georges; 'Georges Noble', 'Georges I', first SOE agent parachuted, March 5/6, 1941; arrested in Villa des Bois mousetrap October 24, 1941; escaped July 16, 1942, returned to London and became SOE Signals officer

Besnard, Julienne, née Simart, then Aisner, 'Claire', recruited by Déricourt January 23, 1943, as his courier; went to London by one of his aircraft April 15/16, for training, returned by another of his aircraft May 13/14, with SOE status; returned to London April 5/6, 1944

Bodens, Karl, 'Anton', agent of Giskes sent to France to impersonate one of captured North Pole agents, with Christmann

Bodington, Nicholas, second in command to Buckmaster; on MTB to receive 'Cat' and de Vomécourt on their passage to London; 1st mission, to south of France, August 1942, conferred with Girard, left on September 9, 1942 by felucca; 2nd mission, 'Alceste' landed by one of Déricourt's aircraft July 22/23, returned to England by another of Déricourt's aircraft August 15/16, 1943; afterwards left Baker Street to lecture on French politics to troops

Boemelburg, Sturmbannführer, Commandant Gestapo HQ, 82 Avenue Foch; his fate is unknown, though it is generally presumed he was killed in Holland during a bombing raid in the latter stages of the war

Bonoteaux, Colonel, member of ORA, landed by Lysander together with Lyon to reception by Déricourt, June 23/24, 1943, arrested by Bony-Lafont gang

'Claire', see Besnard

Borrel, Andrée; 'Denise', 'Denise Urbain'; courier to 'Prosper'; parachuted September 24/25, 1942; arrested June 24, 1943; sent to Karlsruhe May 12, 1944, executed by lethal injection at Natzweiler on July 6, 1944

Carré, Mathilde; The 'Cat', 'Victoire', joint founder (with Czerniawsky) of the Interallié, independent intelligence network working to London; arrested November 18, 1941, used by the Germans to bait traps in which many of her former agents were caught; on meeting de Vomécourt turned back to the British and crossed with him to England by MTB February 26/27 1942; kept in Holloway until end of the war, then handed to the French for trial; sentenced to death; sentence commuted to imprisonment in perpetuity; released after serving twelve years

Cartaud, Pierre; 'Capri', agent of Rémy, arrested June 1942, went over to Germans, attached to Kieffer's staff 84 Avenue Foch, accidentally shot by Germans May 1944

'Cat', the; see Carré

Clément, Rémy; 'Marc', airman, recruited by Déricourt January 26, 1943, as his assistant; he found the airfields for Déricourt and helped in the reception and despatch of aircraft; following inclusion in momentary mass arrest in August went to London by one of Déricourt's aircraft, September 17/18 for clearance, returned by another of Déricourt's aircraft October 16/17, 1943; left to carry on for a while after Déricourt's recall, in his stead

Cohen, Gaston, 'Justin'; parachuted down 1943, radio operator to Robin; never arrested

Cole, Harold; 'Paul', self-constituted agent working with PAT escape organisation, arrested December 11 or close, betrayed some of his comrades then escaped; arrested by Vichy authorities May 1942 and passed into German hands with occupation of Unoccupied Zone; went completely over to Germans later in war; after the war shot while resisting arrest

Christmann, Richard; 'Arnaud', double agent in the service of Colonel Giskes; sent to France with Bodens by Giskes in interest of North Pole, May-June 1943 and November 1943; received post-war clearance from Allies

Churchill, Peter; landed by submarine for two brief missions as 'Michel' in early 1942, and on third mission as 'Rauol' by parachute on August 27/28, on Riviera coast; liaison to Carte; arrested April 15/16; sent to Sachsenhausen (not apparently in the main part of the Concentration Camp with other prisoners)

Culioli, Pierre; 'Adolfe', local Resistant who took over duty of parachute reception, to 'Prosper'; arrested June 21, 1943; survived Buchenwald; charged by the French with intelligence with the enemy but acquitted

'Denise', see Borrel

Déricourt, Henri Alfred Eugfene, 'Gilbert', 'Claude'; airman, left France by PAT escape line, arrived in Britain September 1942, joined SOE in November, parachuted blind January 23, 1943, to take up post as Air Movements Officer; Organiser *Farrier*, controversial relations with Germans; obeyed recall to England February 8/9, 1944; charged by the French after the war with intelligence with the enemy, but acquitted

Dubois, A.; 'Hercule', landed by one of Déricourt's aircraft April 14/15, 1943, wireless operator to several Organisers including principally Frager; shot and killed Scherer November 19, 1943, shot and wounded Vogt in subsequent pistolduel; recovered from his own wounds but executed in Germany

Frager, Henri; 'Paul'; independent Resistant, started in *Carte* network, Girard's second in command until schism; visited London in April, 1943; on return organised network *Donkeyman* in Yonne district, liaised with but independent of

SOE; enemy of Déricourt; dupe of Roger Bardet and of
Bleicher; went to London October 20/21, 1943, returned by
sea end of February, 1944, arrested by Bleicher July 1944;
hanged in Buchenwald October 4, 1944

Garry, Emile Henri; 'Cinema', later 'Phono'; Organiser of
network *Cinema* in Le Mans area; arrested October 18, 1943,
hanged at Buchenwald, September 9, 1944

Girard, André, 'Carte', artist creator of network *Carte* on the
Riviera coast which in 1942 appeared to SOE potentially the
most important in France; fetched to London October 20,
1942 and not allowed to return; finished war in America, where
he settled

'Geoffroi', see Watt

Giskes, Colonel, Chief of German Military Counter Espionage
(Abwehr) in Holland, Belgium and Northern France; ran
Operation North Pole; fetched to England for interrogation
after the war but given a clearance

Goetz, Dr., civil auxiliary and radio expert on Kieffer's staff. 84
Avenue Foch; until the war a schoolmaster; given post-war
clearance by Allies

Guerne, Armel, 'Gaspard', recruited locally by 'Prosper' as his
personal *aide*; arrested July 1, 1943; escaped in January, 1944

Inayat Khan, Noor; 'Madeleine', 'Jeanne-Marie Regnier'; sent out
to supplement 'Archambaud' as radio operator to 'Prosper';
landed by Lysander June 16, 1943; arrested October 13, 1943;
sent to Karlsruhe, Pforzheim November 26/27, 1943; shot at
Dachau September 12, 1944

'Jacqueline', see Rudellat

Kieffer, Sturmbannführer; Commandant of SD HQ, 84 Avenue
Foch former police officer at Karlsruhe; hanged by the British
after the war, some people think wrongly

Kiffer, Raoul; 'Michel', 'Kiki', agent of Interallié, arrested November 1941, turned into agent of Bleicher, organised fake network in Lisieux area of Normandy; condemned to death by French after the war, sentence commuted to one of imprisonment, now out

'Lise', see Sansom

Lyon, Robert, recruited by de Guelis in France, 1941; arrested indirectly through Villa des Bois affair October 24, 1941; escaped July 16, 1942 and went to England; landed by SOE Lysander, as 'Adrian', 'Gilbert Calvert', together with Bonoteaux June 23/24, 1943, to reception by Déricourt, trailed by Bony-Lafont gang as far as address in Paris where gang had orders to follow him no further; proceeded to Lyons, where he became Organiser of network *Acolyte*

de Malval, Baron Henri, 'Antoine', recruited by Basin March 1942; his villa Isabelle became the safe house for agents arriving in France from the Riviera coast; arrested in Paris July 13, 1943; as a result of beating about head lost one eye

'Marc', see Clement

'Marcel', see Agazarian

Norman, Gilbert, 'Archambaud', 'Gilbert Aubain', radio operator to 'Prosper', parachuted November 2, 1942, arrested June 24, 1943, shot at Mauthausen September 6, 1944

Odette, see Sansom

'Oliver', see Basin

Placke, Joseph, member of Kieffer's staff, 84 Avenue Foch, who ran pseudo-Canadian network in north of France; received post war clearance from Allies

'Prosper', see Suttill

Rabinovitch, Adolphe; 'Arnaud'; 'Guy Lebouton', parachuted into south of France October, 1942, radio operator to Peter Churchill; after the arrest of Peter Churchill on April 15/16 went to his lodgings at great personal risk to remove compromising documents; returned to London; parachuted on second mission, March 2/3, 1944 to German reception; executed in Germany 'Robin', see Worms

Rowden, Diana, 'Paulette', courier to 'Bob'; landed by Lysander, June 16, 1943; sent to Karlsruhe May 12, 1944; executed by lethal injection at Natzweiler, July 6, 1944

Rudellat, Yvonne, 'Jacqueline', landed by felucca on Riviera coast July 1942, made her way Loire valley, Tours district; courier first to Flower, with whom she disagreed, then to Culioli, at whose side she was heavily wounded, then arrested, June 21, 1943; never really recovered from her wounds; died in Belsen

Sansom, Odette, née Brailly, later Churchill, now Hallowes; courier to Peter Churchill, arrested April 15/16, 1943; sent to Karlsruhe May 12, 1943, thence to Ravensbrück; driven by the camp commandant to meet the advancing Allies and presented to the Americans in the last days of the war

Scherer, Auguste, civil auxiliary to Kieffer's staff, 84 Avenue Foch; schoolteacher in France before the war; interrogated the couriers, and also Resistants other than French Section; shot by 'Hercule' November 19, 1943

Starr, George, 'Hilaire', Organiser of network *Wheelright* in Gascony, one of SOE's few total successes

Starr, John A.R.; 1st mission 'Emile', parachuted as food expert to 'Carte', August 1942, returned by November felucca; 2nd mission 'Bob', Organiser of network *Acrobat* in Dijon area, parachuted May 1943; arrested July 19, 1943; attempted escape from Avenue Foch with 'Madeleine' and Faye; afterwards gave parole; sent to Mauthausen Extermination Camp, from which he slipped out in May 1945

Suttill, Alfred François, 'Prosper', 'François Desprée', Organiser *Physician*, largest SOE FrenchSection network, covering Paris and most of the Loire Valley; parachuted October 2, 1942; arrested June 24, 1943; executed at Sachsenhausen on March 21, 1945

Turck, Gilbert, 'Christophe', agent of Colonel Humphreys, whom on June 25, 1940 he followed to England; enlisted in Free French July 1, parachuted back on August 8; falsely suspected of implication in Villa des Bois mousetrap, October 1941 arrested July 7, 1942; sent to Buchenwald, then Dora; received post-war clearance from British and French

Watt, Arthur; 'Geoffroi', parachuted October 16/17 as radio operator to Déricourt; returned to London April 5/6, 1944

Worms, Jean, 'Robin'; Organiser of network *Juggler* in the Marne district, parachuted January 23, 1943; arrested July 1, 1943; executed at Flossenburg on March 29, 1945

Vogt, Ernst, civil auxiliary to SD, interpreter to Kieffer, 84 Avenue Foch, former bank clerk; wounded November 19, 1943, returned to work January 1944; received clearances from the Allied governments after the war

de Vomécourt, Pierre, 'Lucas'; 1st mission, parachuted May 10/12, 1941; Organiser *Autogiro*, returned to England with the 'Cat', by MTB, February 26/27, 1942; parachuted back April 1, arrested April 25, 1942

Young, John Cuthbert, 'Gabriel'; radio operator to 'Bob', parachuted May 1943, arrested November 17, 1943, through false 'Benoit'; shot at Mauthausen, September 6, 1944

A NOTE TO THE READER

If you have enjoyed this book enough to leave a review on **Amazon** and **Goodreads**, then we would be truly grateful.
Sapere Books

Sapere Books is an exciting new publisher of brilliant fiction and popular history.

To find out more about our latest releases and our monthly bargain books visit our website: **saperebooks.com**